Lockport Boy

Lockport Boy

---

*a memoir
of a magical time
and place…*

FRANK BREDELL

Andiamo Press

Published by
Andiamo Press
Box 484, Lincoln Park, MI 48146
e-mail: Fbredell@aol.com

+

Copyright 1999 by Frank Bredell
All rights reserved

+

Library of Congress Catalogue
Card Number: 99-96410
ISBN: 0-96748460-0-x

+

Printed in the United States of America
First Edition/1999

+

Typography/Production by
John Cole GRAPHIC DESIGNER, Santa Fe NM

A WORD UP FRONT

W ho gets the credit (or blame) for this book?

First, my three children, Paul, John and Marie, born in that order, are the ones who always had an interest in hearing about my childhood. "Tell us a story about Greasy Walker or Cousin Hugo," they'd say, even though they already knew the stories by heart.

What started here as only a few stories kept growing as I remembered more and more of my own history. It's odd how long neglected memories come back if given a little encouragement.

The writing was the easiest part. After all, who was going to disagree about what I thought or did? But here and there a fact was needed—the name of an almost remembered teacher, the location of a street, and proof that I hadn't muddled up memories of stores and other businesses. To the rescue came several people including reference librarians at Lockport Public Library, creators of two wonderful Lockport web sites on the internet, and a number of former high school classmates who learned of my project through one of those web sites and shared their own memories with me. To all of them I am thankful.

After I had put my words on paper came the hard parts—editing and proofreading the manuscript. Jean Carnahan cheerfully undertook those onerous chores, not only once, but time after time because I kept changing my mind about what I had written. Although she didn't share my childhood, she questioned whether I had exaggerated or even created some of my "memories," and displayed an uncanny knack for ferreting out the truth. Without her help the manuscript would be just a bunch of half-completed stories.

When I thought I was ready to turn typing into printing several friends came to my aid. Ed Sickafus and the Rev. Harry Cook, who had already successfully mapped the tangled thicket of self-publication, shared their knowledge of the technical "how tos" of creating a book. Boyd Miller, also a publisher as well as a former newspaper editor and retired professor of journalism, smoothed out the rough parts of the manuscript, and Thad Brykalski, a long-time friend and colleague, designed the covers and indeed the entire book.

Bob Rooney, webmaster at www. Lockport-NY.com, embarrassed me with the publicity he gave me and my venture on his website, and offered valuable marketing advice.

And along the way, several people who heard that the

work was in progress said they wanted to buy copies of the book when it was completed. That was encouraging, especially since they hadn't yet read a single word of the text and didn't even know what the price of the finished product would be.

To all of these people my heartfelt gratitude.

Frank Bredell

Chapter 1

THE WATERMAN
STREET GANG

We always knew when Uncle Tonius was coming. Not that his car made a lot of noise. In fact, it was very quiet as it drifted down Waterman Street from High Street at about two miles an hour. It was the only car on the street without a driver. All we could see was a brown felt hat protruding up a tiny bit behind the windshield. And there was a wisp of cigar smoke coming out the driver's side window, which was open a crack. The car itself was a bit unusual too. It wasn't old, a 1937 Dodge four-door sedan, quite new in those long-ago days, but the color was something that only the Army could love. They probably took years to develop that dead olive drab look on all their cars, but Tonius' car just got that way all by itself.

But I'm getting ahead of myself. At this point in our wandering tale you don't know who I am, and you certainly haven't been introduced to Tonius. Charles Dickens had a great opening line in David Copperfield. Maybe I should borrow it: "Whether I shall turn out to be the hero of my own life or whether that station will be held by anybody else, these pages must show. To begin my life with the beginning of my life, I record that I was born…"

I don't know when David Copperfield was born, but I arrived in the world May 29, 1930. John F. Kennedy was born on that date in 1917, and going way back, that was the date when Sultan Mehmet II conquered Constantinople in 1453 to usher in the Ottoman Empire in Turkey. But I didn't know any of that until years later.

My mother wrote important stuff in a little brown-covered notebook. The first page reads, "Frank Fulston Bredell Jr., born May 29, 1930. Weight 10 pounds, 1¾ ounces." You couldn't get any more accurate information than that. That page is followed by a careful recitation of the formula I was given in the hospital, what I was fed at home, when I got my first teaspoon of orange juice added to the formula, and when the first bit of cereal was introduced. Boring stuff, but my mother must have wanted to remember it. As it turned out I was to be her only child. I don't know if things were planned that way or it just happened.

Being an only child didn't mean being lonely. There were plenty of other kids in the neighborhood to play with—the members of the Waterman Street Gang. Across the street were Doris and Audrey Donner. Doris was older than me, old enough to be my babysitter sometimes, but more often she was a pal and what people called a tomboy. She had no

The embryo of the Waterman Street Gang.

interest in dolls or girl kinds of things but was good at games like kick the can or stickball. When we chose up teams we all wanted Doris.

Her sister, Audrey, was maybe a year younger than me and had hair like straw. Not just the color, it stuck out from her head like pieces of a bundle of straw. She wasn't as good as her sister in games but was OK, so we chose her, too. Besides, she owned a Monopoly game and we all gathered on Donners' secluded porch to play at least two or three games every week during the summer.

There was a thick vine over one side and the front of the porch, something we called Dutchman's pipe, that had little white blossoms in the shape of pipes. Sometimes while we were waiting for Audrey to decide whether she wanted to risk nearly all her Monopoly money to put a hotel on Massachusetts Avenue the rest of us would each pick a pipe and "smoke" it. The vine also had some thin, dry little branches that broke off easily, so since the blossoms were pipes, we assumed that this had to be the tobacco.

We tried to smoke it once, not in the little Dutchmen's pipes, of course. They were just flowers and wouldn't hold any tobacco. Jack Schuler stole a pipe that his father used to smoke and hid it out behind Jimmy and Howard Garlock's house. He and I nonchalantly broke off a few twigs of the dry vine while Audrey pondered over a Monopoly move.

After a while we got tired of playing and took an intermission. I don't know what Doris and Audrey did, but Jack and I sauntered over to Garlock's and got out the pipe. We rubbed some of the dry curly stems of the Dutchmen's pipe vine in our hands and made a coarse dust that we put in the bowl of the pipe.

Jack had stolen some matches, too, so we tried to light the pipe. The "tobacco" didn't catch so we tried another match. That one didn't work either, so we tried a third. We had to get this right, there weren't many more matches. The twigs started to smoke when Jack lit the next match, and we each quickly took a puff at the pipe.

It was awful, we could hardly breathe. We gagged and gasped for air, then tried to throw up but couldn't. Jimmy and Howard Garlock were cheering us on, very quietly so their mother wouldn't hear. They weren't quiet enough, though. She peeked out the back window and spotted us.

She didn't come out, and we didn't see her so we assumed all along that we were safe. Howard and Jimmy were severely interrogated later when they went into the house, although their mother could see that it was only Jack and me rolling on the ground.

For us, it was now a matter of recovering our wind, cleaning out the pipe and hiding all the matches. Jack and I were still gagging, so Jimmy and Howard gathered up the matches and hid them under the weeds that grew profusely in their back yard.

Finally Jack was able to recover enough breath to take a little stick and clean the remaining "tobacco" out of the pipe, which he then hid in his pocket to take back home.

Fortunately neither my folks nor Mrs. Garlock had a telephone. (I think Jack's parents might have.) Mrs. Garlock always kept to herself so she didn't report our misdeeds to anybody. She didn't have to. Later in the afternoon, when I went home for something, my mother asked me if there had been a fire somewhere. She smelled smoke. I said something about someone on Millar Place burning trash, which she knew was a lie, but she let me get away with it.

I think she had been over to call on Mrs. Donner and Awful Audrey had told about how we had picked the curly branches off the Dutchmen's pipe to smoke. I expect that my mother and Mrs. Donner nearly fell off the porch with laughter while they thought of how awful that would taste. My mother decided I had punished myself enough, so she didn't have to do anything more. None of us ever tried to smoke the Dutchmen's pipe again. As a mater of fact, Jack never again tried to smoke *anything*. We did still strut around with the little pipe-like flowers in our mouths that summer though.

Next to Donners, going away from my house, lived Mrs. Ranney, who had no kids and must have been at least 100 years old, or so we thought. We were all scared of her although she never chased us away from in front of her house. Next to Mrs. Ranney were the Buddenhagens, but their kids were grown up, working and had moved out of the house, so we never paid much attention to them.

Between Buddenhagens and the little grocery store on the corner of Waterman Street and Millar Place was where Jack lived. He was my third best friend after Jimmy and Howard Garlock. (Of course, that order always depended on which of us was mad at one of the others at that particular moment, and that changed from day to day and sometimes from hour to hour.)

Sometimes Jack and I roller-skated in his cellar, around and around the furnace in the winter when we couldn't do it outside. Even though we had fun in his cellar it was a little scary because his father had papered all the walls with newspaper stories about the Lindbergh baby kidnapping. When we were old enough we read some of the stories, which made me think I might be kidnapped. Maybe right out of Jack's cellar. Maybe by Jack's father who had once been in the Navy and had a tattoo on his arm to prove it. He also had coal black hair, a coal black mustache and a very sly grin that made me think he was going to kidnap me.

If I called for Jack on Saturday morning his mother said he couldn't play because he was going to ride his bike to church to go to confession and then had to scrub his grandmother's floor. He was a Catholic. I was glad I wasn't; I did-

My Waterman Street home.

n't want to spend Saturday morning going to confession, whatever that was, and scrubbing my grandmother's floor. In my mind the confession and scrubbing were inseparably linked. Anyway, my grandmother lived 25 miles away and I couldn't ride my bike there to scrub her floor.

I'm not sure how much scrubbing there really was. I suspected sometimes that Jack's grandma was just luring him to her house so she could feed him a good lunch. Jack was pretty skinny. So was I in those days. Jack's church was St. John's, near his grandmother's house. He shouldn't have gone to that church because Waterman Street was in St. Mary's parish. I had learned that much about Catholics from Jimmy and Howard, who were good boys and went to St. Mary's like they were supposed to. Their mother would have killed them if she had found that they had gone to another church, any church, even Catholic. She especially didn't want them going to any Protestant church, so we never took them to any suppers or anything at Emmanuel Methodist.

But back to the houses in the neighborhood. Next to Jack's house was a little grocery store, which was handy to buy a few things when it was open. It seemed to have new owners every few years and would be out of business in between. It never had much stock and so few customers that the vegetables were never fresh and the meat not to be trusted.

On my side of the street, the corner house nearest to us faced Willow Street, so that wasn't part of our block in my reckoning. Anyway there were no kids there, only Mrs. Hulton who had an English accent and would come to visit my mother once in a while.

Between Mrs. Hulton's house and ours were the Kastners. They had a little girl, Alice, too small to be part of the Waterman Street Gang. Anyway, her mother and father didn't want her to be contaminated by the rest of us. There's a whole lot more to say about the Kastners, but I'll get to that later.

The Kastners lived on the south side of us, Edna Stockwell on the north. She was another old lady (maybe 50) who had no children, since she'd never been married. (In those days nobody but nobody ever considered that marriage and having children weren't inseparably bound to each other.) Miss Stockwell never cared when our ball went into her yard, but we sometimes never got it back anyway. Her yard was a jungle of weeds, trees and bushes. Sometimes she'd come out and pull the tops off a few weeds, but never dig out the roots.

Garlocks lived next to her. There was Mrs. Garlock, little and stooped over and always wearing a dark shawl like many hunched over Italian widows in Lockport. Garlocks weren't Italian, they were Irish, but none of us cared anything about that. There must have been a Mr. Garlock at one time since there were five children, Jimmy, a year younger than me; Howard, two years older than Jimmy; Ralph and Rob, both several years older than Howard; and Mary, older than all the rest. She babysat for me sometimes, on the very rare occasions when my folks went out in the evening.

Next to Garlocks were the Plasters. Betty Plaster was just a shade too old to be admitted to the Waterman Street Gang. Living in the houses beyond Plasters were a bunch of people who had no kids. The only one we really knew was Mrs. Workman, and then only because we thought her first name was a scream—Pansy.

All of our back yards were the same size, except that Garlock's was bigger. I suppose it couldn't have been, but it always seemed that way. Maybe because there was a little shed at the far end. It had once been a chicken coop, then storage for tools, and later was sort of abandoned. It was perfect as the clubhouse for the Waterman Street Gang.

First, we needed desks. In those long ago days oranges came in crates made of thin wooden sides and thicker ends. Those would make perfect desks if we could get them, and we could from the little store on the corner. We didn't bother to paint the crates or even sand the splinters off them but just stood them on end for desks. The "chairs" were other wooden boxes from the grocery. Kids now can't do any of this because everything comes in cardboard boxes instead of wooden ones.

No girls were admitted to the clubhouse, of course, so we needed a way to keep them out. We got a piece of cardboard and lettered on it in heavy pencil "Keep Out." We tacked it outside the clubhouse. There had once been a lock on the shed, but it was long gone. The hasp was still there though, so we found a stick that would fit through the loop and hold the door shut. That and the sign certainly ought to keep the girls out and did. We never stopped to wonder if the chicken dirt had anything to do with their lack of interest in coming in.

In the clubhouse we made great plans for projects, games and deviltry. Mostly the club meetings revolved around planning how to get even with the hated Pine Street Gang if they ever attacked us. The backyards of my house and the Garlocks' house backed up to the yards on Pine Street. Somewhere in those houses on Pine Street lurked the menacing Pine Street Gang.

We were never certain, at least I wasn't, who the members of the Pine Street Gang were. I don't think we had ever seen them up close. They also didn't have a clubhouse like the Waterman Street Gang did, so they certainly must have been of a lower social order.

If the Pine Street Gang had ever been identified it might have put me in a difficult spot. Behind our house, on Pine Street, lived the McDonalds with more kids than we could count, some boys and some girls of assorted ages.

Being from different streets, they and I never played together, but just the same, we were over-the-fence friends, and I don't know what I would have done if I'd found out that some of the McDonalds were members of the Pine Street Gang. Fortunately, that never happened.

Howard, being the oldest of our gang members, proclaimed himself president. Jimmy, Jack and I were vice presidents. Since we had no money, individually or collectively, we needed no treasurer. And we didn't plan to keep any records. Heavens no. Everything said in the clubhouse was supposed to be a great secret.

Sometimes, maybe once a week or oftener, Howard exceeded his authority and one or more of us resigned from the gang and left the clubhouse. Occasionally these exits lasted all day, especially if the blowup came in late afternoon. But who else were we going to play with? Not the hateful Pine Street Gang and we didn't want to hang around with Doris and Audrey all the time. The gang soon got back together.

In late September when the days were getting shorter there would be some after-dinner meetings in the clubhouse, if we all had our homework done. Since we all went to different schools, we couldn't do our homework together. Our gang meetings were very serious and very secret. We planned to go "graping." That meant that on a night the next weekend, when there would be no homework to do and we could stay out late (maybe an hour after the streetlights came on), we'd raid a neighbor's grape arbor.

There was always someone in the neighborhood who was growing a few grapes. Jack took it upon himself to ride his bicycle up and down every street within our purview to see what grape trellises he could spot and how big the grapes looked from a distance. Then there was a not-very-learned discussion about the superiority of green grapes vs. the blue ones.

On the given night we met outside the clubhouse. We couldn't meet inside at night because it had no electricity, candles might have burned it down and besides we weren't supposed to have any matches, and flashlights would have been a dead giveaway that we were up to something we shouldn't have been.

We knew the location of our target. Jack usually scoped out whether the grape owner had a dog, and let us know about fences and other menaces. So we set off, slinking along in the shadows until we were near the coveted grapes. Then we tiptoed across lawns and gardens up to the arbor. Somebody had a jackknife. That was usually Jack, because he had a pair of high top boots that came with a little jackknife that fit in a special pocket.

The knife was opened silently, and some bunches of grapes were sliced from the vine. Filling our hands, we ran out of there at top speed, especially if there was a dog barking. The barking added to the fun, our adrenaline was racing, and our hearts were pounding for fear of getting caught. We plunged through the gardens we had been so careful to ease through earlier. Tomatoes were crushed, sometimes a squash got in the way and was kicked to pieces or taken along for no good reason.

Gardeners on Waterman Street seemed to be fond of putting low, almost invisible wire fences around their gardens at ankle height. We almost always got snagged by one of those and fell face down in the dirt. Grapes were scattered and had to be hastily swept together, as much as possible in the dark, and taken away.

Often we split up in making our escapes. We'd learned the value of doing that while watching the cops and robbers movies on Saturday afternoons at the Rialto Theater.

Back outside the clubhouse we slumped to the ground, on the side where Mrs. Garlock couldn't see us, and sampled the grapes. They weren't ripe. We'd come too early again this year, as always. Nevertheless, we all tried to eat a few and proclaimed them excellent. Then we took them out to the street to watch for traffic so we could spatter the rest of the grapes against the back of a truck, preferably a white one.

Waterman Street had very little traffic in the daytime and hardly any at night, so we had to venture over to Pine Street where there were more cars. "Here comes a bus," said Jimmy and wound up his pitching arm. "Don't," yelled Howard, "The driver can see you." So the bus escaped unscathed.

Same thing for all cars. Throwing grapes at them would clearly be too dangerous. Bicycle riders, if there were any, were also off limits. They could hop off the bikes and chase us across yards. Sometimes a truck really did come by and we hurled away at it. Our missiles fell harmlessly in the street to be crushed by the next car, but we'd made a good try. Congratulations were due all around, and we headed for home wondering whether we'd be able to sneak into the kitchen or bathroom to scrub the grape stains off our hands before our parents began to question where we'd been.

Before we went home, we had to plan another foray. "How about next Saturday night?" asked Howard. "My grandmother's having a birthday party, and I have to go," responded Jack. "It's no fun unless we're all here," I said.

By then we were near our homes and departed in separate directions. There would be time at the meeting on Monday to see if we could arrange another rendezvous. If not, there was always next year.

Halloween was another good time to go out looking for trouble. We discussed the merits of throwing tomatoes or squash at someone's front door. Once I even stole a squash and hurled it at someone's steps. When I heard the thud as it landed and watched seeds and squash spatter all over the steps, porch and door, I decided I didn't want to do that any more. What if someone fell on that slippery mess? What if I broke the glass in the storm door? Or worse, what if I got caught and taken home? Besides there were big kids running around on Halloween and Jimmy, Howard, Jack and I were afraid of them even though none of us would dream of admitting any such thing.

We weren't afraid of getting caught by the police during any of our escapades. Lockport's policemen were overage and overweight and seldom left their patrol cars for anything that might involve running or even rapid walking.

The gang wasn't always destructive. Sometimes we did nice things. For example, Waterman Street was once dug up for construction of a new sewer. There was a trench probably eight feet deep and six feet wide all down the middle of the street for several blocks. There were empty oil drums along the edge of the excavation every 20 feet of so, and each was topped with a red kerosene lantern or a flare that looked like a small bowling ball with a knob on it. The knob would be lighted and burn all night to warn drivers.

An old man came around every evening at dusk to light all the lanterns and flares, but once failed to show up. We watched for him until the streetlights came on, and still he didn't appear. Somehow Howard got some matches, from one of his big brothers, I think, and we managed to light one of the kerosene lanterns. We carried that with us to every other lantern and flare, got a little stick blazing and lit all the rest of the warning signals.

The next evening the old man appeared on the scene again. It was clear, even to us kids, that he was still on a bender but had sobered up enough to buy a big bag of penny candy which he gave us as our reward for lighting his lanterns and probably saving his job. We were all proud of ourselves that night and went home to tell the story.

In the summer the days were so long that we weren't allowed to stay out until the streetlights came on. That might have been 10:30 or even later. We'd be called in just as the sun's last rays were dimming. When the days were shorter the lights were the signal to go home or maybe on weekends to be ready to go home in half an hour.

When it was almost dusk it was time to play stickball. I don't recall that there were any rules. We even let Doris and Audrey play, especially Doris. She could hit the ball farther than any of us.

The batter took a position in the middle of the street. Right over a manhole lid was a good spot. Somebody bounced any old ball, but probably a tennis ball that had lost its zip and we had found near the courts at Willow Park.

The batter had a stick, maybe a broom handle or, when times were tough, a branch from a tree. He whacked the ball as it bounced toward him then ran for a place we had vaguely identified as first base and back to the manhole cover. The game was something like baseball or cricket without teams, strategy, skill or good equipment. It sounds like a dumb game. It was, but we enjoyed it.

When we got to stay out after dark it was time for kick the can. There weren't many rules for this either but enough so we could stop the game for long and loud arguments. It was those arguments that usually brought our parents onto the playing area to call the game because of darkness and the players' bedtimes.

In essence, the object of kick the can was to have two teams facing each other, spread out up and down the street and then kick an old empty tin can at each other. Getting it beyond the farthest player scored a point. Playing in the dark made it all but impossible to see the can sometimes because we'd choose a rusty one, and there weren't many streetlights on Waterman Street. If a car came we'd have to stop the game for a moment, but there weren't many cars either.

We could have played softball, but we hardly ever did. Willow Park, with its ball diamonds, was close enough so I could see it from my bedroom window, but there were usually regular teams playing there. There was also a big vacant lot about a block away, and sometimes we played ball there, but the weeds were almost as tall as we were and it was hard to swing the bat and keep track of the ball. We called the place The Jungle.

It was one of our favorite places to explore. We never knew what we might find, like old bottle caps (I had a collection), pieces of ceramic tile left from when there had been a house on the lot, or maybe some broken bricks or colored glass.

Part of the site was a sand hill, a perfect place to take toy cars and build roads and racetracks. It was also good for marble games. Jack, with his high-top boots, ground his hard heel in the dirt to make a shallow hole into which we shot marbles. Sometimes we played for "keeps," but there were always quarrels over that because our best shooting marbles were not the ones we wanted to part with, should we lose.

When all this paled there was always Monopoly on Donners' porch. Jack and I had porches too, with chairs and even a little table, but the games always went on at Donners'. Jimmy and Howard also had a porch on their house, but it was glassed in and too hot to use in the summer.

No matter what we were doing we stopped when we heard the iceman's bell. He came down the street in a covered wagon drawn by a very tired horse who knew the route just as well as Mr. Snow did. That was the iceman's name, which was very appropriate, but we never thought much about it then. Later he got a rickety truck but drove it just as slowly as the horse had walked.

The iceman stopped at nearly every house because we all had iceboxes. A big block of ice would last in the icebox for a couple of days, or maybe longer in cool weather, so whenever anyone wanted ice they'd put a red sign in their window.

The sign was a diamond with a number in each corner, 25, 50, 75, 100. Whatever number was on top told Mr. Snow how many pounds of ice to deliver to that house.

After he had chipped a big ice block into whatever small size was wanted he'd sling the smaller block onto his shoulder with tongs and walk to the house. Water dripped all along behind him, but he wore a thick leather pad on his shoulder to keep sort of dry. When he got to the icebox he'd have to take his ice pick and chop the remainder of the old ice into small bits to let the new block fit.

While he was making his delivery we stood on the wagon wheel hubs and reached in for ice chips. We thought we were getting away with something and Mr. Snow went along with the game, chasing us away when he came out of the house. We never caught on that we were only eating the chips that couldn't be sold and would soon melt anyway.

I wanted to be an iceman when I grew up. Or maybe a coal man. That was even better, listening to the coal rattle down the big metal chute into the coal cellar. What a grand career I'd have. I realized that the ice and coal businesses might be seasonal, so I thought I'd be a dentist in the off season.

Our fun with Mr. Snow and his ice wagon ended gradually as our houses got refrigerators, one after the other. But by that time we were much too grown up and sophisticated to be climbing up on a truck or wagon and stealing ice chips.

Whether the iceman cometh or goeth, the Waterman Street Gang had to soldier on, but we needed some distinctive vehicles. We supposed that the Pine Street Gang had bicycles, so we needed something different, something better, something we could build ourselves. Scooters!

First we had to round up the parts. Needed: one roller skate, preferably one on which the wheels would still turn even if a bit balky, a 2 x 4 board about three feet long, an orange crate and a smaller board. The orange crate was no problem, and the clubhouse or my cellar yielded suitable boards. Luckily somebody could always locate a skate. I didn't want to sacrifice one of mine because they were still in good condition, but I think the older Garlock brothers may have been reckless with their things. By rummaging around in their stuff Howard could come up with one skate that had no mate.

These were not in-line skates, mind you. Their wheels were like those on a car, two in front and two behind, and made of hard steel that made lots of noise on the sidewalk and eventually grew flat spots that made skating even more of an adventure than the bumps in the pavement. The skates had no shoes of their own. They simply clamped to the bottoms of our leather shoes and were held tight by a threaded bolt that was tightened by a skate key.

If you lost your skate key you were in trouble because the skates always had to be tightened about every five or ten minutes. We wore skate keys on shoestrings around our necks. One good thing about those skates was that they adjusted for various sizes of shoes, so we didn't outgrow them.

To make a scooter we had to cut one skate in two so that we had two sets of wheels. For that we needed a saw or a hammer and chisel. My dad had those things all neatly hanging up over his workbench in the cellar but I didn't think I could take any of them outside. Jack's father apparently didn't care. Or maybe Jack could sneak them out so his dad wouldn't find out.

Skates, as we learned, were made of very tough steel. The two sets of wheels were meant to stay together and stay they did despite our best efforts with saw or hammer and chisel. We took turns sawing and swinging the hammer and watching the sparks fly as the steel chisel smashed into the skate. Little by little we dented the part of the skate that was supposed to go under your foot and eventually it would come apart, leaving jagged edges behind that usually gave us some minor cuts, but such was the price of invention.

If we were lucky we could find a 2 x 4 about three feet long, but if necessary we had to hack it out of a longer board. The skate pieces were nailed to one of the wide sides of the board, front and back. Then the orange crate was nailed upright on one end and a little board nailed across the end of the orange crate to make a "steering" handle. This whole operation, as simple as it sounds, would take us a whole day to achieve, or maybe more because we had to interrupt it for Monopoly games, meetings in the clubhouse, safaris in the jungle, etc.

Once completed, the scooter could be propelled like any other scooter, with foot power. It didn't run as well as a store-bought scooter with big rubber tires and smooth handles, but it was ours. We made a second scooter if we could find more parts, but if we couldn't duplicate our efforts we had to take turns riding the one scooter. The Pine Street Gang had nothing that even came close. At least, we didn't think they did. How could they have even conceived of such a wonderful invention? We never went over to Pine Street to see if they had stolen our technology.

Such were our summer activities, but, like the Olympics, we had winter games as well. At the first heavy snowfall of the winter I'd bundle up in snow pants, heavy jacket, scarf, mittens and knitted cap that could be pulled down to cover my whole face. I was ready to face the Yukon or join Admiral Byrd, but I could scarcely walk under all those clothes. On really cold days, when it got around zero, I'd have on two pair of pants, a heavy plaid shirt and a homemade sweater under all that gear. I had to get outside quickly or I'd dissolve in a puddle of sweat.

Jack, Howard and Jimmy were all dressed the same way and we waddled together with our sleds to Ferguson's. That was the name of some people who lived on Willow Street only a couple hundred feet from my house. I don't remember ever meeting the Fergusons, but they must have been kind people, letting all of us go sledding in their back yard.

The yard was a hundred miles long. Well, maybe not quite that long, but our sleds could hardly ever get to the end of it no matter how much of a start we got. The Ferguson house sat on top of a little hill, and the back yard was one long endless (to us) slope with a little trickle of a stream near the bottom that was sometimes, but not always, frozen. The trick was to stop the sled just before reaching the stream.

We took turns pushing each other at the top of the hill, and then the rider tried to steer the sled into virgin territory. We carefully compared the length of the tracks of each run to see who went the farthest. These computations were by no means easily made. We had to take into account the variable conditions of the snow, the different slopes of the hill, the necessity to dodge around bushes and whatever other excuses we could find for not breaking the "world record." Sometimes the disagreements over the calculations got so vigorous that one of us took his sled and went home in a huff. Of course, that didn't usually last too long because once home there'd be no one to play with.

If I went in the house covered with snow I was immediately stripped of all of my various outer layers of clothes, which were hung up to dry in the cellar. Getting all that stuff back on was too much work, so the choices were to get over being mad and go back to the hill or call it quits for the day and maybe get put to work dusting or running the vacuum cleaner or some such miserable chore. Guess what won out.

After traffic had packed down the snow, Waterman Street was like glass. The city didn't dump salt or ashes on our street as it did on some of those that carried more traffic. The slippery street was the perfect place for us to go "slamming." We hugged our sleds to our chests, ran along the street until we got to top speed (difficult with all those clothes that we were forced to wear) and then slammed belly down on the sled. Sometimes we went half the length of the block, and with a Flexible Flyer, the best kind of sled, as we all knew, we could steer and even do spins in the street.

All of this depended on the lack of traffic, but in that we were quite blessed. Once in a while a car hooted its horn and we had to get out of the way. More dangerous were the times that Mr. Dawson, Lockport's assistant fire chief, roared out of his driveway at top speed to answer an alarm.

When I was a kid Lockport had snow. Serious snow. Keeping the walks shoveled was a major undertaking. Maybe once every two or three years it snowed so much that school was closed, but unless we had to plow through drifts more than waist high, school went on as though nothing had happened. I never gave a thought to how teachers managed to get to work. They just did. That's what they were supposed to do.

After a big snowstorm our driveway didn't get shoveled for several days. My dad never drove the car to work. He walked and came home from the bakery only to shovel away at the driveway until he was exhausted. During the day my mother was out there toiling, and I flailed away with a shovel, too, for whatever good that did.

Down the street from our house was a water pump—the big green, cast iron kind of affair that every farmer had in his yard. Why it was on Waterman Street in the midst of houses that had been built in the 1920s I have no idea. Certainly Lockport had running water in every home and there was no need for a well and pump unless it was to give water to the horses who still pulled the ice, bread and milk wagons.

There were other wells around too. Every evening Mr. Donner came out of his house with a pail, walked over toward Willow Park and came home with a pail of well water. I guess he didn't like the taste of the city water, which we kids always told each other came from the canal.

I was never able to get "our" pump to work, even by hanging on the long handle. Sometimes Jack, who was stronger than I was, was able to get a stream of rusty water from it. Even if we could have made it work better, we wouldn't have tasted the water. We knew it was "poisoned." Some of the kids weren't as smart as Jack and me, however. Bob Shimer, who didn't even live near us, remembers coming to Waterman Street with a strong friend who pumped him a good steam of water, which Bob drank. Then the friend reminded him about the "poison." Bob went home and waited to die. After a couple of days, when he hadn't even gotten sick, he decided that he'd been spared, but never sampled the pump water again.

He tells of another incident involving the pump. He egged on one of his friends to put his tongue on the handle during a cold winter day. The tongue stuck, of course, and a neighbor had to be called to bring a teakettle of water. A similar incident appears in a movie about a kid growing up in the 30's, but Bob Shimer alleges that his story is factual. He says that was the same victim who got dragged into the pit under a farmer's outhouse when it was tipped over one Halloween.

Our childhoods weren't dull, even though we didn't have such things as televisions, rock music and the internet to entertain us. We weren't deprived. At least none of us thought we were. Our fathers were working even during the depression, except for the Garlocks, whose father must have died when Jimmy and Howard were quite small. They never talked about him.

We were a mechanized gang. I started with a tricycle, moved up to a scooter (homemade, then store-bought,) and then to a bicycle. All of us had more or less the same equipment. The tricycle came for my birthday when I was five, a fine, big-wheeled conveyance. I was so proud of it I immediately wanted to take it on a long trip, so checked out with my mother to see if it would be OK for me to make sandwiches for Jimmy and me to go on an extended adventure. She guessed it would be all right as long as I didn't turn any corners or cross any streets. That effectually limited me to ride on Waterman Street to the corner of Price Street, a block away. Jimmy checked with his mother and got an OK too, so we both invaded the kitchen at my house and made peanut butter sandwiches, which we wrapped in a used bread wrapper.

Onto the bikes. Mine was so shiny the glint would have blinded passersby, of which there were none. Jimmy's machine was a hand-me-down from Howard so had lost a bit of its luster but not its attraction for him. We sallied forth to the corner of Price and Waterman and dismounted. Hungry after that grueling effort we sat under a big maple tree and ate our sandwiches.

After examining our vehicles to see that they hadn't suffered any damage during the long trip we returned home and reported to our mothers, who said they had been worried sick about us. Nevertheless, the journey was repeated many times.

When I outgrew the tricycle my folks gave me a secondhand red bicycle with medium skinny tires. That extended my cruising range considerably, especially since by then I had permission to cross some streets. Now I could ride down to Jack's house or even to the store next to his house for a few groceries that I carried home in the bicycle's wire basket.

When we all had bicycles we launched "war games." Our first weapons were little white berries, a little larger than peas, that grew on bushes in Donners' yard. By running our hands down a branch we picked off a handful of the berries all at once. Of course, we denuded the branch of its leaves, too, but we didn't ever worry about that. The berries weren't fit to eat, even by birds, but they were fairly firm and were good missiles when thrown. We threw handfuls at each other while we rode around on our bikes.

But we needed some something better. You know what countries do in an arms race, they keep getting more and more powerful weapons. We moved on to pea shooters, little hollow tubes through which we could blow to propel small objects. We tried dried beans. Too uneven in size, some got stuck. Peas, despite the name of the shooter, weren't good either. Dried split peas were too small and our stores didn't have any other kind. We settled on pearl tapioca, small pellets as hard as rocks. Did they ever sting when we got hit by them.

The proper technique of using a pea shooter was to take a whole mouthful of tapioca, being careful not to swallow any, put the pea shooter lightly to the lips, ride along on the bicycle to a likely target and blow away. With a little practice what skill we developed. The ground became white with tapioca pellets.

Our mothers hated the pea shooters and tried to get us to give them up. That stood as much chance as the anti-gun lobby has against the National Rifle Association. Their next ploy was an attempt to get us to reduce the caliber of our ammunition. My mother suggested that we switch from tapioca to rice, and gave us a bag to use. "You'll put someone's eye out with that tapioca," she warned. Why do mothers always think something that is fun will put someone's eye out? They never say, "That'll take somebody's ear off." No, its always the eye.

We tried the rice, each of us putting a handful in our mouth. We blew mighty blasts, and the rice just dribbled out the ends of the shooters. The grains were too little. We refused to sign our mothers' "Geneva Convention" about the weapons of war and reverted to tapioca. Now the Pine Street Gang had better watch out. We were armed.

Oh yes, bigger adventures were coming, but time at that age dragged on so slowly. Every year was like two. Now every year is like a day. It doesn't seem fair.

On our expeditions around the neighborhood we always kept a sharp eye out for the mailman. His arrival twice a day (yes twice) was a big event, not just for us kids, but I think for our mothers who were home, too. We called the mailman Jess. Whenever we saw him we'd make finger guns, draw quickly and shoot him, proclaiming proudly, "Got you, Jess." He'd also make a finger gun and in his gravely voice say back, "Got you, Jess." He called us all Jess. I suppose it was easier if we all had the same name. Lord knows how many other Jesses were lurking around waiting for his arrival on other parts of his route.

Twice a day he emptied the mailbox on the corner of Waterman Street and Millar Place. It was a heavy iron box about two feet high, a foot or so wide with a little slot in the top. It was painted Post Office green and fastened to a telephone pole.

Mailmen (there were no mail women) in those days walked their entire routes twice a day. There was none of this sissy stuff of using cars or trucks for part of the trip. Of course, junk mail had yet to be invented. Jess and his colleagues launched off from the post office on East Avenue, maybe the one where my father's Uncle Frank had once presided as postmaster.

The only time a mail truck came down the street it meant that somebody was getting a package. Fortunately the dark green trucks made enough noise so that everyone could come to a window and peek out to see who was getting a delivery.

"What do you suppose is in that box?" my mother said. "You don't think Mr. Donner bought a new suit when they went to Buffalo last week? He could have. The alterations would be done about now. How do you suppose they could afford it? That Whitmore Company must pay him a lot of money."

Mr. Donner drove a truck for the Whitmore Company, which sold crushed stone and other building materials. Mr. Donner always came home looking very dusty, but we all had the idea that he made lots of money. If he did we had no idea what he spent it on. The Donners' house was no bigger than ours, their car was just as old, they never took vacations, and never entertained except maybe one or two friends. Mr. Donner didn't drink (or if he did, we kids never knew anything about it.) He didn't smoke either. Maybe his Lutheran religion didn't let him. Our mothers, of course, never drank or smoked. The Donner family dressed plainly, just like everybody else we knew in Lockport. Their big extravagance was sending Doris and Audrey to the Lutheran school.

On Waterman Street everybody seemed to have about the same amount of worldly goods and we all lived about the same way. Those were the days of the Great Depression, and although we weren't aware of it we were much better off than a lot of people. We ate well, went on picnics, got out the car once in a while to just drive around in the nearby countryside, took a week's vacation in the summer somewhere in New York State, and lived the good life. It all seems pretty simple now, but enticing.

The Lockport *Union-Sun & Journal* was a skimpy paper, and as a kid I never read anything but the funnies, so I didn't know about the dust bowl, the Oakies, bread lines, men selling apples on street corners of big cities, or the strutting of Hitler in Europe, and the coming war that would turn all of our lives upside down.

Our only vague impression that there might be something wrong with the economy (we didn't know the word, of course) was the presence of an occasional beggar in the neighborhood. We called them tramps, maybe because they were always walking. They came one at a time, never in pairs. Shabbily dressed men, they knocked at the back door, took off their caps and politely asked for food if we could spare any. They seemed to be very used to being turned away and just moved on looking sad and tired, limping as though they'd walked a long way whenever they were refused a handout..

Quite often my mother made them a sandwich. After all, my dad worked for a bakery, and we always had plenty of bread in the house. He could bring home the day-old stuff, which was still plenty fresh. Usually there was some baloney or cheese to make the sandwich for the tramp. He sat right down on the curb out in front and ate whatever he was given.

Most of the tramps offered to work for their food, but my mother never asked them to do anything. She didn't want them hanging around any longer than necessary. They looked kind of scary to me as they peered out intently from behind shaggy beards and wore clothes that they had probably picked out of a junk can somewhere. They smelled bad, too, but I suppose their only bath came from standing out in the rain.

There may have been other signs of poverty around, too, but as kids we didn't see them. We took things as they were, thinking that was the way they had always been. Our parents had lived through the booming twenties and probably were aware of the business slump and unemployment of the thirties, but I never heard them fret over it. Sometimes they'd talk about the fun they'd had in the good old days before I was born, but never in the kind of way that made me feel that I shouldn't have intruded on their lives. I felt wanted and loved. I guess all of us kids on Waterman Street did.

Chapter 2

LOCKPORT: CENTER OF THE UNIVERSE

In History

Now that you have begun to learn a little bit about my neighborhood, you should probably also learn something about Lockport, where this great saga took place.

Being the cultured, well-informed, intelligent (add any more adjectives that will make you feel good) person that you are, you may already know all about Lockport. In the 1930s, 40s, and even the 50s it was, as St. Paul said about his hometown, "no mean city." Lockport is in New York State but not that part down in the southeastern corner that is known to all who live there as "The City." As though there aren't cities, too, out in what those City folk consider still to be the Indian lands.

Lockport is in the northwest corner of New York. Find the place on a map where lakes Erie and Ontario come close together. There's a river connecting them, not a very long river and pretty useless for boat traffic but important all the same because it has Niagara Falls in the middle of it. The land to the east and north of Niagara Falls is called Niagara County. It fits snugly up in the corner of the state. You'd think that Niagara Falls, the biggest city in the county, would be the county seat, wouldn't you? But you'd be wrong. It is Lockport. How that happened, I'm not sure, but I think it always grinds people from Niagara Falls to have to go to what they consider dinky Lockport to do business at the County Courthouse.

In a way it was Niagara Falls that created Lockport. There was a great plan, cooked up in the early 1800s, to build a water route connecting New York City with Buffalo. Part of the trip could be made by rivers that were navigable, but there was the matter of getting over the escarpment, the cliff that created Niagara Falls and which extends east for many miles.

In 1807 newspapers in Western New York carried a series of letters to the editor signed only "Hercules" that argued that a canal linking the Hudson River with Lake Erie would permit grain to be shipped cheaper from the midlands to New York City instead of by wagon or down the Mississippi and around Florida by Atlantic coastal steamers. Farmers and trappers in the Midwest would benefit from lower shipping costs, consumers in the east would, it was argued, have lower prices, and, a major selling point, the tolls collected by the state would pay for the canal.

The Niagara County Department of Tourism claims that it was a resident of Lockport, Jesse Hawley, who suggested the idea of a canal. Since Lockport didn't exist until the canal was being built, according to the same brochure that credits Hawley, this claim needs more investigation, but let's press on anyway.

New York Gov. DeWitt Clinton liked the canal idea and got the legislature to put up money to start construction in 1817, despite scoffers who decried the project as "Clinton's big ditch."

Lockport was still a wilderness, but nevertheless land speculators moved in and bought up the territory where they thought locks might be constructed to get boats up and down the Niagara escarpment. Sure enough, the locks were put right where these 20 speculators were buying land.

Construction of the locks began in 1821, and the village of Lockport was born. The next year it became the county seat, and a courthouse and jail were built in 1825. The canal builders recruited 1000 laborers, and merchants moved in to supply them with food, clothing, shelter and various types of amusements. (Maybe some of the amusements created the need for the jail.)

During the building of the canal Lockport was a village of log cabins erected close to where the work was going on. Sometimes too close, as many houses had to be protected by log walls from flying rocks sent into the air by blasting. The mostly Irish laborers recruited to do the heavy work had little experience with the black powder used to dislodge the stubborn limestone. One historian remarked that it was difficult to get experience in the blasting business because people working with the powder didn't live long enough to become experts.

In 1825 Lockport had 2500 residents, the same number as Buffalo and Rochester. The Erie Canal, as it was named, was opened by Gov. Clinton October 26 that year when he boarded a boat in Buffalo which was tugged along by mules to New York. The governor, knowing a photo-op when he saw one, dumped a barrel of Lake Erie water into the Atlantic Ocean in a ceremony he called the "Marriage of the Waters."

The canal was a large undertaking for its day but not of great size by modern standards. The locks at Lockport were 90 feet long, 15 feet wide and four feet deep. Boats could carry 75 tons of freight. The canal was enlarged twice in later years, and the present locks are 328 feet long, 45 feet wide and 12 feet deep. Boats can carry 2000 tons of freight. (Just thought you'd like to know all the numbers.)

The canal was a hit with the farmers and traders. It had cost $100 to ship a ton of goods by wagon from Albany to Buffalo, but with the canal the cost dropped to $10. And enough tolls were collected so that the canal turned a profit 10 years after it was opened. Coincidentally, the City of New York began to boom at the time the canal was completed and all because of the locks at Lockport. Just stand in the middle of Times Square today and ask anyone if the Erie Canal and Lockport didn't cause New York's prosperity. No one will know what you are talking about.

When the canal was finished, people thought Lockport would die, but the settlement kept right on growing, thanks partly to the electricity generated by a sluiceway that had been built next to the locks.

A Lockport inventor of the time, Birdsall Holly developed an underground water pumping system, complete with hydrants for fire protection, the first in the country, and in 1865 Lockport had the first fire company in the world—Hydrant Hose Company Number 1—that was equipped to use the hydrants.

The fire protection system made Holly world famous even though he was a social outcast in Lockport. He had divorced his wife and remarried. It was a shocking and unheard of thing to do in the 1850's, especially to marry a woman 28 years younger than himself. Shocking! But business was business, and Holly's fire protection system really caught on. Chicago failed to buy it and burned down in the Great Chicago Fire. The city bought Holly's system immediately after the fire.

Holly installed a central steam generating facility in Lockport and sold steam to heat homes and stores in the downtown area. This invention, too, caught on with other cities, after a few problems were solved. In Lockport the water for the system was drawn from the canal, and a few fish and other debris clogged the pipes. Some screens and a man to clean them eventually took care of that.

Officials came to Lockport from New York to see Holly's steam generating system and bought it. After that the Lockport factory could barely keep up with its orders.

Holly, by the way, had more patents than anyone at the time except his friend Thomas Edison. The Holly company remained Lockport's leading industry until 1904, although Holly had died 20 years earlier. Superstitious people will like this: the night of his death the village of Gasport, near

Lockport, burned down. It was one of the few cities that had failed to buy Holly's fire hydrants.

After the Holly industry moved to Buffalo, other industries moved to Lockport and slowly filled the gap. The most successful of those was the Harrison Radiator Co., which made honeycomb auto radiators invented by Herbert C. Harrison, a Lockport native. "Harrison's" (now Delphi-Harrison Thermal Systems, formerly a part of General Motors Corp.) is still Lockport's biggest industry and major employer.

Other big names in Lockport's history include William G. Morgan, who invented volleyball; and Belva Bennet Lockwood, the first woman lawyer admitted to practice before the U.S. Supreme Court and the first woman to run for president of the United States (1884 and 1888 as the Equal Rights Party candidate.)

Among other political luminaries was William E. Miller, Lockport native who ran for vice president with Barry Goldwater. He didn't make it, fortunately, so no more need be said about him.

Back on the industrial front, the first commercial production of aluminum took place in Lockport in 1888, but an argument and lawsuits between the inventor and his Lockport financier resulted in Lockport losing the company that became Alcoa.

See, I told you that Lockport was "no mean city."

But back to the early days of the city, when it was only a village. The canal locks built at Lockport had to raise Buffalo-bound boats fifty feet to get over the escarpment. The original town of Lockport was built as two settlements because of that escarpment—an "upper town" along the higher level of water toward Buffalo, and a "Lowertown," the name it still has, beneath the locks.

The two areas competed to be the center of importance, but eventually the upper town won out, especially when the canal was enlarged in a project that lasted from 1841 to 1860 (politics can mess up anything.) The reconstruction cut off the waterpower that gave rise to Lowertown's mills, and that part of Lockport began to decline in importance.

The canal was enlarged once again, in 1918, a project that saw the original five locks replaced by the present two. Eventually, however, railroads and trucking companies stole the canal's business, and the present canal is mostly a pleasant place for owners of small boats who want to avoid the waves on nearby Lake Ontario.

Only 25 years after the Erie Canal opened Lockport was a thriving community. It had 22 dry goods stores (today there are none downtown), 15 groceries (hardly any downtown now), eight saw mills (all vanished), three banks (now there are none that are locally owned), three book stores (all gone now), two gun factories (fortunately also gone), a glass factory (it hung on for quite a while, but is now out of business), a cotton mill (gone), and other businesses.

By the time of the Civil War Lockport residents were quick to volunteer for the Union army. In fact, the first Union volunteer was William Bush, a Lockport saloonkeeper who organized his customers into a platoon of which he became captain. (I'm not making this up, it comes from no less an authority than the Eastern Niagara Chamber of Commerce.)

Even before the end of the war Lockport had begun to grow. It became a city in 1865, the first in Niagara County, the first telephone was installed in 1879, and in 1885 there were streetlights and door-to-door mail delivery. Before all of this, the first commercial telegraph message in the world was sent—from Lockport to Buffalo in 1845. Yes, you historians will claim that the first message was sent by Samuel F.B. Morse in 1844 from Baltimore to Washington, but that was only a *demonstration*. The real business started in Lockport with the report of Lockport's election results.

In my memory

Joyce Carol Oates, a fiction writer who was born somewhere out in the wilderness just west of Lockport, wrote once in the *New Yorker* that she always remembers Lockport as though she is looking at it in a sepia-tone print.

I never managed to read all the way through one of her books, but I guess she has a point when she describes Lockport like looking at a brown antique photo. Maybe it is because the city doesn't seem to change much, yet at the same time a lot of it is new. Downtown was totally destroyed by "urban renewal," which meant that the classy old buildings were demolished and nothing was built on their sites. Businesses that survived the demolition moved to the south end of Lockport, outside the city limits, to create a wasteland of commerce. Lockport's old timers mourn the passing of downtown.

Main Street was alive and well when I was growing up in

the 1930s and 40s. The *really big building*, a skyscraper all of six or seven stories high (depending on how you count the vast first floor) was the Farmers and Mechanics Savings Bank on the corner of Main and Locust. Now, that was a bank! A big, solid looking building with lights all around the top. I had a savings account there and once in a while would march in with my mother or father and have my interest entered in a little passbook.

I never could quite figure out how they knew which three dollars on deposit was mine. I supposed that my money had a little drawer all of its own, and I imagined it in a cellar, under the sidewalk which had little glass-like circles in the pavement to let a bit of light down to brighten up my money. I always wondered who was down there taking care of it.

The 10-cent stores were the really cool places to go. You could find "everything" there and in the days before I had any money except my allowance I'd do my Christmas shopping there.

My mother did her important shopping at the two department stores, Williams Brothers and the Carl Company. Williams Brothers was the stodgier of the two, and the atmosphere inside was more like a tomb than a store. Voices were hushed as though every transaction was a secret. The displays were boring to me, but I loved the way the clerks took the money and put it in little baskets that ran on overhead wires to someplace out of sight where change was made and a receipt prepared. You had to stand at the counter for maybe up to five minutes while all this took place, and the clerk had to be polite and stay too.

At Carl's pneumatic tubes served the same function. (Or maybe I have the two devices confused, and it was Carl's that had the little overhead baskets on wires. Both stores are long gone now.) Carl's also had little yellow stamps that could be pasted into a book after every purchase, and a full book might be worth as much as $5.

Williams Brothers had its own clothing label, and when you saw one you knew that the quality of the goods was excellent. A customer once bought two untanned fox pelts from a trapper and took them to Williams Brothers to have a stole made. Williams Brothers did it for a charge of $8. That was in 1954.

Lockport in the 30s and 40s had three movie theaters in or near downtown. The best, and most expensive, was the Palace, conveniently next door to the high school for those who wanted to cut classes. The first-run movies played at the Palace, and we always felt that we should be quite dressed up to go into those faux marble halls.

The Rialto, a little closer to Waterman Street, was where I went more often. It had Saturday matinees with a double feature (one picture always a Hopalong Cassidy, Tom Mix or other Western) and a serial—a continued story with a new chapter every weekend. It was amazing the scrapes those actors could get into at the end of the episode, but by the next week it was all solved in a couple of minutes, leaving plenty of time for new heroics. One of my favorite Christmas presents was a long string of tickets, worth 10 cents each, for the Rialto. On Saturday afternoons I'd go with one of my friends and sometimes even give them one of my precious tickets.

There was one other theater for a time, the Hi-Art, on West Main Street near the Niagara Bakery where my father worked, but the legend among us kids was that there were rats running around the Hi-Art, often over people's feet. We never went there.

Kelly's meat market was near the theater, and my mother did shop there. There was sawdust on the black and white tile floor and big fans whirling overhead. This was the day before any stores were air-conditioned. The meat was either in the long refrigerator cases or hanging in a cooler behind the counter. If my mother said she wanted three pork chops the butcher in a long white apron and straw hat lifted a huge loin of pork out of the refrigerator, laid it on a chopping block and cut off the three chops—always holding the pieces up for my mother's inspection and discussing how thick the chops should be cut.

All this time I'd be eyeing the colorful jars of sauerkraut and various varieties of pickles on the shelves and enjoying the cool breeze from the fans. Sometimes it was worth a visit to the store just to get cooled off.

Most of our other shopping was done at the little groceries in our neighborhood, but once in a while there was a need to visit a "supermarket." There was the Mohican or the A&P. Neither was nearly as big as my school classroom. We usually went to the A&P because it had fresh vegetables in bushel baskets on the floor and boys who would carry the groceries out to the car, but most shopping for fresh produce was done at Scirto's Fruit Store, where everything was sold in bulk. Of course, in the summer it was easier to just drive a few miles out in the country and pick up things from stands in farmers' front yards. That was (and still is) one of the joys of living in Lockport. You are never far away from fresh fruits and vegetables.

Sometimes we went to a nearby farm for raw milk. I don't know why we did that except that it was much cheaper than the milk delivered to the door by Wyles', Castle's, or Gascoyne's dairies. All those dairies were cheaper than Randleigh Farms, which alleged that its milk was superior to all others. Its dairy was fun to visit, though, even if its milk did cost too much. From the ice cream parlor you could look through big glass windows and see the cows being milked down in kind of a basement by very clean and modern machinery. And you were protected from cow smells, besides. The ice cream was the richest anywhere and the most expensive.

On East Avenue, in the midst of a very nice residential street, was a fish market, Montondo's. How it got into that row of elegant homes I don't know, but it may have been the same way the auto paint shop got into Waterman Street. The neighbors felt sorry for a young couple trying to start a business, so they never objected.

I don't remember ever going to Montondo's. My mother didn't like to cook fish and so whenever we got the urge for fish, which was about once a month, we went to a little restaurant out in the fields north of Buffalo. The place was called The Syracuse, but we always just called it the fish house because the building looked like a simple house with a big neon sign shaped like a fish on the roof.

The fish came with a golden crust, a piece so big it hung off both sides of the blue plates it was always served on. Then there was a mound of potatoes, a big heap of vegetables, and a large side dish of coleslaw. All this for 75 cents.

The place was always busy, and you could understand why. We got to know the best times to go to avoid standing in line. Maybe they took reservations, but for years we had no telephone, and even when we did have one that would have been a long distance call and probably would have cost as much as a fish dinner. Besides, we didn't really understand all the technology of making long distance calls, getting an information operator in another city and especially trying to remember the real name of the restaurant. Picking up the phone and saying, "Gert, get me the fish house," wouldn't have worked anywhere but in the movies.

When he was working for the Niagara Baking Co. my dad came home for lunch, but later, when he was driving a bus he'd often have lunch at a little downtown Lockport spot that also got to be a favorite of mine when I was on a summer job working for the City of Lockport Street Department. It was named Aldrich's but usually called Mother Aldrich's, for the woman who ran it. She was assisted by her two daughters, one in the kitchen and one waiting on tables. They did all the cooking and baked their own pies in the morning.

The little restaurant had a counter with about four stools and three or four tables, which were always shared by anyone who came in. The restaurant was a little wooden shelter that sort of clung to the outside of a substantial brick building. If the restaurant had ever let go its hold it would have slid down Market Street into the canal. Maybe that's what happened. It is gone now.

Food was plentiful and cheap at Mother Aldrich's—about 65 cents for an entrée, vegetable, soup *and* salad, home-made pie and coffee or tea. When the price went up to 75 cents Mother Aldrich went to each customer and apologized at great length for the increase. The clientele included a few men whose wives had more grandiose notions of cooking than Mother Aldrich's simple menu. They often requested meat loaf, macaroni and cheese and similar things. She always obliged. I put in a request for chocolate pie, which found its way onto the menu several times. Mother Aldrich always saved me a big piece.

Otto Plaster's newsstand was an institution. It was run, of course, by Mr. Plaster, who lived just three houses down Waterman St. from us. His daughter, Betty, used to baby-sit for me when I was little, but that didn't cut any slack with Mr. Plaster, who was as grim as a judge and gave every customer a stern once-over as they came into the store. We always had to be on our best behavior and say a polite hello to Mr. Plaster, who always answered, "Hmmmph."

The store had *all* the magazines that were published, but many of them were under the counter where only Mr. Plaster could reach them. My friends and I never dared ask for *Sunshine and Health*, a nudist magazine with a few black and white photos taken at a great (and disappointing) distance from a group of scrawny nudists playing volleyball. Once in a while we found a copy that some adult customer had perused and failed to hand back to Mr. Plaster. We went over the issue page by page until Mr. Plaster snatched it away. Then we bought a 10-cent comic book, just to show that we had business being in the store and to avoid being kicked out for all time.

The store had wonderful old squeaky wooden floors, and on the cigar counter was a little metal tube from which shot out a tall flame at the press of a button to light cigars. The store was small and narrow, but nevertheless there were always a few Lockport "senators" present and in session discussing the weighty topics of the day.

Lockport was filled with little corner grocery stores and bars. My dad delivered bread to most of those in the west end of Lockport and in Lowertown. Children of Italian immigrants ran a lot of them, or they were operated by the old people themselves who spoke Italian to many of their customers. Lockport had many descendants of the Irish who had come to build the canal, quite a few Italians who had settled there later, and a smattering of blacks, whose ancestors may have escaped from slavery by the Underground Railroad, which apparently had supporters in Lockport.

The city had more Catholic churches than it needed for a town of its size, but there was one mostly Irish, another Italian and several that were built just to serve their own part of the city when parishioners came on foot or in carriages.

On the east end of Main Street, across from the high school, was the library built with funds donated by Andrew Carnegie. It was architecturally imposing and still looks that way although much expanded. The children's library was on the lower level, so we never interfered with the studious adults upstairs. I rode my bike to the library about once a week, especially in the summer when the school libraries were closed. I loved to prowl around the open shelves and find books, especially stories about dogs, or mysteries. In those days before air conditioning anywhere except the movies, the library lower floor was cool and a nice place to spend part of a hot summer afternoon.

When I got to be about 12 my parents thought I was big enough to explore some of Lockport further afield on my bike. I rode all over Uppertown but couldn't cope with the big hill that separated "our end" of the city from Lowertown. Exploring there had to wait until I could drive a car.

The airport was only about a 10 or 15-minute ride away, and one or two friends and I would pedal out to look from a distance at the grounded Piper Cubs that were waiting for their owners to save up enough money for gas. There were no commercial planes. Once an airplane arrived that offered to take people up over the city. The fare was based on the passenger's weight. I wanted my dad to take me, but he figured our combined weights and decided that the money could be better spent.

Lockport had (and still has) some large, elegant houses, mostly on Locust, Willow and Pine streets, not far from Waterman St. They were quite a ways economically, but not in distance, so I checked them all out quite often.

Still in a mood for grandeur, I'd ride around the county courthouse, a large and stately Victorian structure that looked the way a courthouse should.

As an antidote to the grand houses and the courthouse, I'd cruise around the little shacky houses on Caledonia St., some of which seemed to face the railroad tracks instead of the street. At one time my dad was the executor of an estate that included some of those houses and he had to make rounds to collect the rent. If I went along he made me wait in the car. I don't know if he didn't want me to see the insides of them, or whether he thought I'd be an unwanted intrusion in the lives of the tenants, which I certainly would have been.

The canal at Lockport is less than 50 feet wide. A Little Leaguer could pitch a ball across it. There were several bridges across the canal throughout the city, but one was supposedly the widest in the world. It was, of course, less than 50 feet long, but about a city block wide. There was a historic marker on it, but the state decided to call the bridge "one of the widest in the world." Where was their civic pride? We always just called it the Big Bridge.

On the north side was the fire station. When there was a fire alarm the trucks roared out of the station and made a great sweeping curve over the bridge to aim in the right direction. It was the perfect spot for a fire station, and a perfect spot for me to sit astride my bike and wait for the trucks to dash out with much ringing of bells and blowing of sirens. People unfortunate enough to be caught walking across the bridge, which was really only a great expanse of pavement, scattered in all directions, not knowing which way the trucks would finally go. It was one of the best free shows in town.

Since the assistant fire chief lived across the street from us, he took my school class on a tour of the fire station once in a while to show us how he could slide down the brass pole and jump into his waterproof pants with the boots attached. There was a fire alarm bell at his house that rang loudly, but only for major fires. When it clanged he roared out of his driveway just as fast as the trucks did downtown, but Waterman Street being rather narrow, he couldn't make a great sweeping turn at full speed the way they did. Because he might have to go at any time his driveway was always cleared of snow, no matter how deep it was. His wife did much of the shoveling, sometimes climbing up a stepladder with each shovelful of snow to toss it over a snowbank.

Out on the far northwest side of town, almost beyond my bicycle range, was what had once been a camp of some sort. In the middle was a big weedy parade ground, and at a distance were concrete slabs where tents or cabins had stood, a spring that flowed with safe (at least we thought it was safe) drinking water, and thorn-covered paths through the underbrush. The old camp was a good place to explore, and one year the YMCA used it for a day camp, which I attended, riding out each day with my lunch bag. I suppose the secluded spot, reachable down a dirt lane, might have been more popular with an older crowd at night, but I was too naïve to even think of such a thing.

Lockport was a grand place to grow up in the 30s and 40s. It was sort of like Huck Finn's hometown on a more modern and larger scale. I had freedom to explore in safety and security. I feel sorry that the present generation of kids can't share something like that.

Chapter 3

LIFE WITH
MOTHER—AND FATHER

My parents, especially my mother, didn't realize how busy I was with gang meetings, Monopoly games, explorations of the neighborhood and so forth. She thought that I should put that aside and help her with some of her work.

She had a weekly routine, and I had to join in, especially in the summer when I was home from school. Monday was wash day. The washing machine was in the cellar, so all the dirty clothes had to be carried down there.

The washing machine was a big round tub with a wringer on it. If you don't know what a wringer is, go look up a picture of one in an old dictionary or encyclopedia. After the clothes were swished around vigorously in the washer for 20 minutes or so, she fished the pieces out with a cut-off broom handle and fed them one at a time through the turning

49

rubber rollers of the wringer into a laundry tub of cold water. After that they went back through the wringer into another tub of water, and finally through it one more time into a basket on the floor. Sometimes I helped pull the clothes through the wringer, but never fed them in. She was afraid I'd get my hand in there and it would be crushed.

My next job was to carry the basket to the back yard, where there were clotheslines strung in back of our garage. My mother and I hung each item on a line, pinning it with wooden clothes pins. This went on winter or summer, as long as it wasn't raining or looked like rain might be coming. In winter the clothes froze and were like stiff boards when taken down from the lines. They melted and got flexible when taken back into the house and by some miracle, even though they had been frozen, they seemed mostly dry. In summer they came down from the line very easily and were dumped into the empty basket.

Tuesday was ironing day. Our kitchen was too small to set up the ironing board, so the ironing was usually done in the living room. If a neighbor dropped in—and people did drop in unannounced in those days—the board was whisked away and the hot iron placed on the kitchen cupboard to cool.

Twice a year it was time to take down the living room and dining room lace curtains to be washed. What an ordeal that was. We used a kitchen chair to get up high enough to take the curtain rods off the wall. The curtains then could be slid off the ends of the rods. Washing was done in the machine, but the curtains weren't subjected to the wringer, they were just squeezed a little dry by hand.

What a dapper couple—Mom and Dad.

Then came the time to put them on the curtain stretchers, which resembled a medieval torture device. The stretcher was really a big wooden frame the size of a curtain panel and had little nails with their sharp points poking out about every inch all the way around. The device was adjustable, and so the curtains had to be measured when dry and the stretcher set for the right size. Unless it was tightened carefully at the four corners it sagged into a trapezoid shape, which would have left the curtains in a very odd state.

The wet curtains were placed on the protruding pins, which held them stiff and tight when they were completely fastened.

After one curtain was on the stretcher another could be added over it, then another and another until the little pins were full. In the summer this whole apparatus was set up in the back yard, where it was subject to being blown over and the curtains getting dirty. In winter the attic was the drying room.

Another day of the week was vacuuming day. Small throw rugs were taken outside and thrashed within an inch of their lives. With the vacuuming came dusting, including every molding, windowsill and other surface. I had to crawl down on the dining room floor and dust the ornate legs and braces of the table, buffet and china cabinet.

Saturday was baking day. Never mind that my father worked for a bakery and could bring home day-old goodies galore. My mother made her own, especially big white sugar cookies and dark brown molasses cookies. When cool they were put in an earthenware crock and were usually served as dunkers at breakfast. She sometimes made mincemeat cookies and other kinds as well, little German Pfeffernüse at Christmas, and sugar cookies shaped like stars, wreaths and trees.

My mother also canned her own fruit and vegetables. We drove to a stand out in the country—about three or four miles away—and bought bushels of peaches, pears, plums, and tomatoes to bring home to can. I brought the empty jars up from the cellar, a bushel basketful at a time, and she washed them. There was no such thing as a dishwashing machine. A dishwasher was a person. Always had been, always would be as far as we were concerned.

She canned by cooking the fruit or vegetables on the

stove in a big open kettle, filling the kitchen with steam. It seemed like the weather usually turned hot, sometimes 90, on canning day. Except once, and I'll tell you about that.

I didn't find out until years later that her "open kettle" method was frowned upon by home economists who thought it would allow bacteria to enter the food and make it spoil. We didn't know that and never got sick. Maybe out of a whole summer's canning there would be one jar that didn't seal properly and would spoil.

The filled jars were placed on dishtowels spread on the counter to cool. After several hours, or more likely the next day, my mother turned over each jar to test it for leaks, wiped it with a damp cloth and put it back for me to label with a date I wrote on a little sticker and applied to each jar. Then the jars had to be toted to the cellar, again in a bushel basket, and arranged in neat rows on shelves that my dad had made for that specific purpose.

I remember just as though it were yesterday one occasion when she made chili sauce. She made and canned a batch almost every year, but the year I remember was special. For a change the weather on canning day was cool, but she had a kitchen window open a little way to let the steam out and some fresh air in. The jars were cooling neatly on the kitchen cupboard and my mother and I sat down at the kitchen table for lunch. The cupboard was behind me.

Suddenly the cool air must have hit one of the hot jars, and it broke. It didn't just fall apart, it exploded, sending hot chili sauce all over my back. Fortunately I was wearing a fairly heavy cardigan sweater. I stripped that off with the speed of lightning as the hot sauce penetrated. As it turned out, the burns were very superficial. A little cold water was the only treatment they needed, but we both learned something: don't let a cool breeze in on the jars. And just to be safe, don't sit next to them and eat lunch. After that we cleared away the usual clutter from the dining room table for lunch on canning day.

I remember the day our living room and dining room traded places. It was during World War II when heating oil, like almost everything else, was rationed, and we had the choice of heating a few rooms to a comfortable temperature, or being cold in the whole house. I suppose my mother and father made a decision about that, but I wasn't there for the discussion. The first thing I knew about any proposed changes in our lifestyle was when I came home from school one winter day and all of the dining room furniture was gone. In its place were the davenport, chairs and lamps that had always, until that day, been in the living room.

The big radio was still in the former living room because it had a permanently attached antennae wire that went out a little hole in the wall, up the side of the house and over to a pole at the end of the back yard. The radio was fixed in place, apparently just like the programs that it brought into the living room, the same ones year after year.

The living room carpet hadn't come into the dining room with the furniture, because it wouldn't fit in that smaller room. The dining room carpet had stayed, but all the furniture that used to stand on it had picked up and gone into what until that morning had been the living room. My mother had single-handedly moved everything including the dining room table, which seemed to weigh a ton, and the three-person davenport that weighed another ton. The china cabinet and buffet had been emptied of dishes and transported as well. The only thing that had stayed in the dining room was the drop-front desk and the huge fern that stood on a wrought iron stand and had grown to be almost three feet in diameter.

The idea behind all of this shifting was the fact that the dining room had French doors that could be closed to separate it from the living room and the hot air register in the living room could be closed, depriving that room, the stairway and upstairs hall of warmth. The only bathroom, upstairs, was heated as usual, but to get to it we had to dash through the icy living room and up the stairs. The bedrooms upstairs had a little bit of heat, but they never had been very warm. For some reason the builder of the house had installed only one heat pipe to serve two bedrooms, and a small pipe to heat the little room that probably was supposed to have been a baby's bedroom.

I liked the shift of the furniture. The small dining room (now living room) was cozy and had none of the chilly drafts that usually came down the open stairway into the living room.

I don't remember how long we lived backward like this, but it probably was less than a year. The dining room was too small for a Christmas tree, and we always had a big tree in the living room, so we must have turned the house back to rights by the following Christmas.

The big shift from living room to dining room wasn't the only time that my mother engaged in an orgy of furniture moving. Every once in a while she rearranged the living room, moving the couch from here to there, putting her favorite rocker in one place then another. Some of this was necessary to clear space for the Christmas tree, but sometimes she just got bored with the layout and made changes. The big radio had to stay in its corner until it was finally retired and replaced by a table model that needed no permanently installed antennae. The other part of the living room that couldn't really be used much was the corner just in front of the stairs. It was too drafty, and so it was given over to a small desk and a glass-front bookcase that held books that no one would ever open, such as a home medical book far out of date, and boring novels that had long since dropped out of vogue.

I never did my homework at the little desk, which was really too small and in that drafty location. I took over the dining room or kitchen table.

The desk did have a function, though. On Friday nights when my dad brought home his pay, in cash and much of it in change, my mother and dad pulled chairs up to the desk and opened the bottom drawer. Inside were small glass jars, each with a label—insurance, gas, oil, electricity, church, etc. That was the budgeting system. Coins clinked into each jar, and a few dollars were stuffed into those that required big money.

There were usually some IOUs in various jars that had to be coped with. Insurance might have borrowed from oil last week, and had to be paid back. Sometimes the discussion my mother and father carried on over the jars got quite animated. There must have also been a jar labeled miscellaneous, because sometimes there were surprise purchases, like the little red metal-clad radio my dad bought for the kitchen. It was placed on top of a metal cabinet and needed about 25 feet of antenna wire draped all around the kitchen to make it work. There must have been something wrong with it, though. Every time I touched it I got a mild shock.

In my bedroom I had a better portable radio that gave no shocks. It only needed about a dozen feet of antenna wire, which was hidden behind the curtains. I listened to the radio turned down very low when I was supposed to be asleep. It was fun to see what far away stations I could get, like New Orleans or Chicago. This was AM radio. FM hadn't yet arrived in Lockport, but we were all happy with the radio reception we had. Maybe that "snap, crackle and pop" cereal slogan was written by someone who was also thinking of the radio reception wherever he lived.

The 30s , 40s and 50s have rightly been called the "golden age of radio." At 5:30 Sunday afternoons, from Labor Day until Memorial Day, was the time for *The Shadow.* I can still hear that announcer say, "Who knows what evil lurks in the minds of men. The Shadow knows." This was followed by a ghastly chuckle that made me shiver and be glad I was safely in the house. The voice may have been that of Orson Welles, who played the part of The Shadow for a few years in the 30s, but radio scholars differ on who said those words.

The Shadow, I have just recently learned, first went on the air in 1930, only four months after I was born, but I doubt if I was a fan yet. When I first heard the show, though, I was hooked and thought that we should most certainly patronize the sponsor, Blue Coal. I insisted even after we started heating the house with oil.

Tom Mix, sort of based on the real cowboy character, was another of my radio favorites, especially that gravelly-voiced character known as the Old Wrangler who always managed to get in my favorite line, "Let's get to goin'." The sponsor was Ralston, a hot cereal that looked and tasted like cooked sawdust, but if Tom Mix said I should eat it I'd try to choke it down. Tom Mix even offered premiums for box tops, so that clinched the deal. I had to eat enough boxes to get a toy gun or badge.

Little Orphan Annie also gave away stuff, like decoder rings if I drank the awful tasting Ovaltine, which I did and sent in the can labels. With the ring I could decode Annie's secret messages. Darn, they always said stuff like "Annie says, 'Be sure to drink Ovaltine.'"

There were lots of other shows that I listened to, like the scary *Hermit's Cave.* Every show opened with a sepulchral-voice warning, "Turn out your lights." I never did, I was already too frightened by what was to come.

Daytime hours on radio were given over to "soap operas," so named for their soap company sponsors. My mother wasn't a daily fan, but she sometimes listened to *Ma Perkins* and as a consequence washed our clothes in Oxydol. And she could fret over that no-good husband in *Backstage Wife* and have a good cry during *The Romance of Helen Trent.*

The Goldbergs was our "ethnic" show, since Molly Goldberg was supposed to be Jewish. Whenever she entered the scene she'd sing out, "Hello, is anybody?" I give the same greeting even now when I go into the little pharmacy where the druggists are hidden behind their cabinets.

A lot of the soap operas began with classical music, probably since no royalties had to be paid to long-dead composers. It was my first taste of the classics, and when I hear some pieces now I can still hear the announcers introducing those old radio shows. And if there was yet such a thing on the market as Blue Coal, I'd like to buy some. I have no idea what we'd do with it in a house heated by gas.

My friends and I all shared the same programs but not together. We seemed to think that we had to be home to listen privately. I could have used the little radio in my bedroom but hardly ever did. I turned on the big living room Philco and shared the programs with my mother and dad, whether they wanted to hear them or not.

In the evenings there were real family programs, like *Fibber McGee and Molly* and *Amos and Andy*. The latter was so popular that no one made any phone calls during the show, and cities noted that water use dropped dramatically. You couldn't leave the living room to go to the bathroom because you might miss something.

It was indeed the Golden Age of radio. I didn't have a television until 1956, when I bought one to watch the presidential election results. What a waste. Eisenhower won again.

As I said, the old upright Philco radio stayed in its assigned spot in our living room for many years, never moving because of that attached antenna wire. Other furniture had no such permanent locations. The shifting of the living and dining room furniture during the war was a one time event, but there were other big furniture-moving extravaganzas every spring when the porch furniture was lifted down from the loft of the garage and every fall when it was put back there.

The biggest item on the porch was a metal-framed glider. After the cushions had been removed and stored, the frame was light enough so that two of us could hoist it up or down from the loft. We only had one stepladder, so I went up to the loft and maneuvered the frame so that my mother could steady it from the ground and keep it from crashing down. Then the two of us carried it to the porch.

The chairs were big metal affairs that were very heavy, but I was able to wrestle them up and down by myself. Then there was the little table made of rattan. Pier One would die to have something like that in its inventory now, but back then it was just some old cast-off that probably once had seen better days and been in a living room. It was painted dark green every once in a while.

The porch was shaded by rolling blinds made of thin slats of wood. Those had to be taken down from the loft, spread out on the grass and sprayed with the hose before being put up. One went in the front. That was the east side of the house, which was shaded by a big maple tree, so the blind wasn't really needed for the sun but more for privacy. The other blind was on the south side of the porch, but definitely for privacy. It was there to block our neighbors, the Kastners, from our sight and us from theirs.

Even after all of the furniture was brought from the garage loft and installed on the porch in the spring, that wasn't the end of the work. About every two weeks my mother drained buckets of soapy water out of the washing machine after she was done with the laundry and swabbed the porch floor and steps with them. Then it was my turn to drag the garden hose from its usual place of repose in the back yard or alongside the driveway and rinse everything down.

Then there was the garden to be dug in the spring. It was a plot about 15 by 30 feet at the end of the yard where my father planted tomatoes and other vegetables on one side, and my mother put in flowers at the other. She also put a few morning glory seeds on both sides of the garage door, and we had strings going from the ground to the eves, then up to the peak of the garage roof. It was a race to see which morning glory would reach the peak first. They really were gorgeous in the morning with their bright blue flowers, which closed later in the day when the hot sun hit them.

Grass cutting was my chore as soon as I could manage the mower. There was no such thing as a gasoline powered mower, at least not in my neighborhood. The weekly cutting was always a good workout and involved a lot of geometrical planning to figure out the best way to cut around the rose bed and the little strips along the driveway and next to the house.

Trimming the hedges that lined both sides of our property was my dad's job until I was old enough so that he trusted me to do a decent job. Like power mowers, electric hedge trimmers were a thing of the future, too. The tool of choice (the only one possible) was a pair of large shears that were heavy and hard to work.

My dad usually spent much of every summer on a ladder painting our house. It was much more complicated than just brushing on a new coat of paint. The last coat, whenever that had been applied, had blistered and flaked off, making the house look like a victim of measles. So my dad attacked one side of the house every year, sanding and scraping until the wood was bare. Then it got a coat of primer and two coats of finished house paint. It took all summer to do one side of the house in this fashion, so the project took four years. By then it was usually time to start again because that paint didn't stick well either. No other house in our neighborhood had paint that peeled like that. Joe Volshaw, the builder who had erected several of the houses in our block, couldn't figure out why ours was the only one that needed constant scraping and painting. The obvious answer would have been to cover the wood with some kind of siding, maybe like the shingles on Donners' and Garlocks' houses. This was discussed over and over again, but apparently there wasn't the money to do it.

Sanding and scraping boards while standing on a tall ladder can be boring and exhausting, so one year my dad brought in a special tool to help—a blow torch. The hot blue flame shot out the tube and the apparatus must have weighed four or five pounds. Now he had to have the blow torch in one hand and a putty knife scraper in the other, with no hand left over to hold onto the ladder. The procedure of blistering the paint with the torch was dangerous. We always thought that the flame would work its way under the wooden siding and set the house on fire sometime during the night. It never happened, but we always stayed home every evening after my dad had been blow-torching, just in case a smoldering fire broke out.

No matter how long or hard my dad worked on his burning, scraping and painting project, no one was invited—or permitted—to help, especially not me. No one could have done it good enough to suit him, so he struggled along by himself. That's why it took four years to make the full circuit of the house.

I have pictures of the house when it and I were both new. My mother is out in front holding me in her arms, and behind her are cascades of spirea bushes, all in blossom. They grew about five feet high and bowed low to the ground, making a great cascade of white flowers all across the front of the house.

Although the effect was spectacular, it didn't last. My dad decided that those bushes would be in the way whenever he wanted to paint the spindles of the porch railing and the wood between the ground and the porch floor. Consequently he trimmed the bushes into tall sticks with a little corona of green and a few blossoms at the top. They were as ugly as you could imagine anything, and he knew it, but in answer to any protests from my mother or me he'd just say, "I might want to get down in front of the porch and paint it this year." Every four years he did, so the bushes remained spindly sticks that did nothing to hide the ugliness of the lower part of the porch.

Life wasn't all work for any of us, of course. I had friends at the house almost every day, neighbors often dropped in to see my mother, and once in a while Esther Leaderhouse walked up from downtown. I guess Esther and my mother had worked together at the bank before I was born and kept in touch. Esther was "a maiden lady of a certain age" as we might say, and decidedly prissy. She held her teacup just so, always.

She hated cats, especially ours. Whenever Esther was due my job was to capture the cat and put him outside, if I could. Usually the wise cat hid and we assumed that it was already out.

Esther arrived after work and perched gingerly on the davenport, afraid that the cat might be lurking somewhere. Finally, since the cat hadn't appeared, Esther relaxed and sat back a bit, as much as would be ladylike. Then the cat made its move. It appeared from nowhere, leaped on Esther's lap, climbed up over her, and zoomed down behind the davenport and disappeared. Esther was terrorized, and it took quite a time to quiet her. Meanwhile I searched again for the cat, but no cat was to be found.

Eventually, when all was again tranquil, the cat made another dash and leap, but this time I was quick enough to catch it as it went beneath the davenport where no one could reach it. The cat was tossed out, but Esther remained on full alert until my dad drove her home about eight o'clock. It had been quite an evening for all of us.

Chapter 4

CHRISTMAS

It was the Christmas season, 1937. Or maybe 1938 or 39. It didn't matter. The ritual never varied from one year to the next. My teacher, a different one every year but always taking full advantage of the season, got us busy right after Thanksgiving making paper chains for Christmas trees, paper snowflakes to put in the windows, and whatever snowy pictures she could coax us to draw.

My picture always included a house like ours — two stories with two windows downstairs, two up, and always a red chimney set at an angle to the pointed roof. I never could draw the chimney right. It always stuck out sort of sideways but had a curl of smoke coming from it. That detail may have been right. Almost everyone in our neighborhood heated with coal then (later to be converted to oil), and there must have been wisps of smoke coming from chimneys lots of times.

65

The important things about getting ready for Christmas took place at home, not in school. There was a strict routine that began several weeks before the holiday with the making of fruitcakes. My job was to assemble the boxes of raisins, bags of candied fruit and dates, the big mixing bowl, and bread pans for the great day. I was allowed to do some of the stirring, too, after my mother had dumped in all the ingredients, but the batter quickly got too heavy and unwieldy for my puny arms, and she had to take over again.

Then came the baking of Pfeffernüse, little German cookies flavored with anise that were hard when they came from the oven but over a few weeks gradually softened, if they didn't all get eaten first. They were carefully laid in a crock and covered with a dish towel, but I had to test them quite often to see if they were softening. The only way to do that was by eating one. Usually I wasn't quite sure of the results so had to try two or three.

There was always shopping, but that must have been done somehow when I was at school. I don't remember going on any big expeditions to buy gifts, but I was only intent on what presents I'd get anyway. When I got older I trudged up and down Main Street in Lockport trying to find the "perfect" gifts for my mother and father. This was tough without much money to spend.

A week or so before Christmas there was the tree trimming. My father brought home the tree in the back of the bakery truck, always a live balsam. Where he bought it I never thought to inquire. It was always a big tree, too high to fit into the living room without a piece of the top being chopped away.

My father wrestled with the tree stand, a three-legged affair that had to have a nail driven through it and into the bottom of the tree trunk to steady the tree. Then a little brass water bucket was connected to the tripod. Keeping it full of water was my job, one that had to be done religiously at least once every day.

The Day of the Tree was usually a Sunday afternoon. I couldn't wait to get through dinner, but everything had to be done in order, and dinner was first. Finally it was over. Then I ran to the attic and carefully brought down the ragged boxes of ornaments. The attic was freezing, so I did run, but the boxes were exactly where they had been resting since last year, so there was no searching about. The only possible trouble was that I might back up into the curtain stretchers. I tried to keep well away from their pesky nails, but sometimes they attacked me anyway. No matter, the ornaments had to come down.

The next order of business was for all of us to take off our shoes and put on slippers. Mine were soft soled, so that when I stepped on a Christmas bulb or something, it might not break. My mother also had soft slippers, usually some I had bought her as a present the Christmas before. I was dying to get out the new ones I had bought her for that year, but that would have spoiled the routine.

My father's slippers were leather with hard soles. He said they had to be hard because he might have to go outside while he was wearing them. I didn't know why he'd have to go outside while putting up the Christmas tree, but then if

I questioned anything I was told that the way things were was the way they were—and would stay that way. I didn't want hard-soled slippers like his anyway, being quite willing to step outside in the snow in my soft-siders and come in with slippers and feet soaking wet. This caper was always followed by a short lecture, but it never did any good.

The tree lights had to be tested. Bulbs were screwed into the first strand of wire in whatever colors came to hand. They'd all be rearranged later. The job now was getting 12 bulbs that all worked. They didn't, of course. In those days unless all the bulbs lighted, none of them did. One bad bulb and the whole string stayed dark. What was it called? Being wired in parallel or series? I learned that in shop in junior high school, but since they don't make that kind of Christmas lights anymore (at least I hope not) I have forgotten.

So the lights wouldn't go on. We'd try another string and another until, if we were lucky, one string would light up. Then we would take every bulb from the dark strings along with the spare bulbs and substitute one at a time for a bulb that we knew was good. This tedious exercise continued for what seemed like hours. Bad bulbs were thrown in the wastebasket.

Oh, I forgot to mention. Before any of this happened, probably on the previous Saturday afternoon, my mother and I would rearrange enough furniture to make room for the tree and lay down a big sheet for it to stand on. The furniture would be shoved where it would be in the way, but there was no other place for it.

Finally, miracle of miracles, all of the little pointy lights and the bulb shaped like a snowman were working. Even the big star for the top of the tree glowed. My mother and father put the lights on the tree. I wasn't allowed to try anything so technically challenging.

Each string of lights was in the shape of a big circle, not one long wire as they are now, so it was tricky to place the bulbs so that they were spaced out and not hanging on the tree in twos.

Next came the ornaments, and I was allowed to participate in that momentous task, with due supervision, of course. Certain ornaments had certain places. We all knew that. Some unbreakable ones and a few that were so ugly and worn looking that we all hoped they'd finally break this year, were relegated to the lowest branches of the tree where the cat could swat at them. The cat did too, when he wasn't sleeping under the tree or trying to climb it.

The climbing, often performed during the most crucial part of getting Christmas dinner on the table, would bring my mother screaming from the kitchen and my father would slap a newspaper to chase the cat. After setting the cat off in a chase throughout the house he would tell me to catch it (how?) and put it outside. After a few minutes of disrupting everything and everybody, the cat would go to the door and plead to be let out of the confusion. I think my mother wished she could escape that easily.

When the tree was all decorated the sheet on which it stood was wrapped around the bottom to try to conceal the ugly tripod standard. The wrapping failed, and every time anyone passed the tree they stooped over and tried to snug up the skirt. It was sort of an exercise in imposed modesty, but the tree and stand always had some nudist tendencies.

The tendencies were most apparent as the tree began to shed its needles, quite soon after the ordeal of the decorating. Many an evening when all was quiet, my father absorbed in his newspaper, me in a book or homework, and my mother knitting, we'd hear the patter of Christmas tree needles falling like rain. Most of the time the tree still looked presentable on Christmas day, though. My mother always hoped for a dark Christmas so that the lights, which were kept on all day, would look pretty.

One year, when I was very small, my parents thought they'd entertain me by plugging the tree into a little gadget that made all the lights blink off and on. It must have been pretty—for a few minutes, until our next door neighbor arrived and began to bellow that the blinker was ruining the reception on his radio. The little blinking device stayed in the box of Christmas lights for years after that but never got plugged in again.

On most evenings the tree wasn't lighted until about five o'clock when it began to get dark. A master extension cord was plugged into the wall socket and all of the multiple tree wires were plugged into it in one huge mass of plugs. It was a wonder that the whole works didn't go up in flames. At the magic moment of light-up there was usually a failure of some kind. Most of the lights came on, but there was one dark string.

Then someone, usually me, had to take out a bulb that had proven to be good and exchange it for one bulb at a time in the string that was dark to find which bulb didn't work. Quite often it would be the 12th and last bulb tested. Do you suppose those bulbs got together during the night and decided which of them wouldn't work the next time the tree was plugged in?

This kind of testing by substituting bulbs continued for years. It was the only way to do it. And then one day my father brought home a little gadget that looked like pliers except that the handles were kind of a hard cardboard and there were jagged points that squeezed together. By putting the points behind each bulb, with both wires in the jaws and squeezing, the current would be diverted and all the other bulbs would light if the bulb being tested was the bad one.

Now instead of taking bulbs out of their sockets I merely had to squeeze the little device behind each bulb until I found the dead one. Technology was wonderful!

As I said, in the weeks leading up to Christmas I shopped through the stores on Main Street to find suitable (I thought) presents for my mother and father. One year I decided that at least one of our living room lamps ought to be replaced by something modern, and so I went to all the furniture stores in town, two or three, and discussed lamps with some forbearing owners. All the lamps were too expensive, so I had to settle for something else. Probably slippers again for both of them.

My father thought Christmas was an ordeal. He never said this, of course, but he was right about a lot of it. On the day before Christmas he went to work far before daylight, even earlier than usual, but didn't get home until seven or even eight o'clock that night. On other days he was home in mid-afternoon, but on Christmas Eve the bakery had special orders to be delivered. Apparently many of the city's lodges planned Christmas parties and had their turkeys and hams roasted at the bakery and delivered. They also needed extra baked goods including fancy decorated cakes. Those often required my dad to make a special trip from the bakery, driving about five miles an hour so the cakes wouldn't shake apart.

It was a long day, and my father arrived home pooped. I'm sure he wanted to go directly to bed to prepare for the next day's ordeal—Christmas at home with the relatives—but, of course, he couldn't do that. I'd been waiting for hours and hours for him to come home so we could open presents. We always opened them Christmas Eve because of the chaos that Christmas Day brought, but more of that in a moment.

Before the presents, though, we had to have supper. I'd been home sneaking Christmas cookies, so I didn't care about the supper; I wanted to get to the presents. My dad, of course, was starved. Christmas Eve supper was always the same, oyster stew that my mother had made and which was always preceded by a little dish of raw oysters. I hated both. I tried them but couldn't get either down. I did have a little of the oyster broth, even though I didn't much care for it, and then maybe a sandwich or canned soup. I was too excited to care what it was.

Whatever I ate that night was always followed by a frosted Christmas cookie (or several) cut in the shape of a tree, star or bell and coated with red and green sugar. My mother had labored mightily a few days earlier and had put by a large crock of those for the holiday.

After several hours, as it seemed to me, supper was finally over, but now the dishes had to be washed. No presents could be opened until the dishes were done. There would be problems enough tomorrow without having to contend with a sink full of dirty dishes first.

So the dishes were washed, dried and put away. Then step two: find the cat and put it outside. That usually wasn't too hard to do because the cat would be asleep on a hot air register, most often in the dining room, where it would absorb all of the heat meant for the room.

Step three, put on the slippers. Step four, get scissors and a large wastebasket. After this long and frustrating exercise in unnecessary delay we were ready to open our presents. By now I had discovered that Santa could make some of his rounds early, so I never questioned any more why he came to our house the day before Christmas.

Finally I had scissors poised to cut the first ribbon. Ribbons were always to be cut, not torn. That's just the way things were. But before that my mother would say, "Frankie," (she sometimes called me that although I hated it) "see if you can get some nice Christmas music on the radio."

Over to the big upright Philco I marched. The thing stood almost four feet high on its curved and carved legs. There was a little postage stamp-sized opening that lit up when I turned the smallest knob. By rotating the largest knob I could make numbers scroll by in the little peek hole opening, from 55 (WGR in Buffalo) down to scratchy

WEBR (owned by the *Courier-Express* in Buffalo), passing the wavy WHAM in Rochester, and ending up with some rumbling noises of WKBW around 150. The old reliable WBEN, owned by the Buffalo *News*, usually was broadcasting carols by this time of the evening, so that's where the dial settled, somewhere in the middle of the numbers.

I fiddled more with the big dial to get the least interference, then one of the medium sized knobs to set the volume, tweaked the other mid-size knob to vary the tone. Changing the tone always seemed to upset the volume, so more careful adjustments were needed. There was no such thing yet as FM radio, no television, of course, or tape recorded music and absolutely no CDs.

Just good old AM radio, noise and all. We thought it was wonderful, and sometimes late at night I could even bring in very faintly a station playing jazz in New Orleans or WGN in Chicago. On Christmas eve we settled for something easy to find with decent music.

Finally we were ready for the presents. As an only child, and spoiled at that, there was package after package for me under the tree, and I dove in but was very careful to cut, not break, the ribbons and put all the paper in the wastebasket, which soon overflowed and had to be taken to the cellar to be emptied into a big barrel. My father did that. He had the hard-soled slippers on. And I was too busy cutting the next ribbon.

Once there was a Lionel 0 gauge electric train, in other years more parts for it, such as a realistic whistle. Those were still the days of steam engines on real trains and whistles that sounded like whistles should, not the kind of fog horns that trains have now.

Once there was an erector set but never a chemistry set. "Too dangerous, you'd blow up the house," my parents told me. I loved toy cars, so there was often another of those. Once there was even one with a wind-up motor so that the car would race around the living room terrorizing the cat.

Always my mother had knitted mittens and quite often a sweater. I never figured out how she did that knitting while I was home but never saw her making them. I did see her making things, but I never caught on to what she was really doing.

I was so involved in my own presents I had no idea what my mother and father gave each other. I think their best presents came later that night when I could hear mysterious noises from their bedroom. But I never figured that out either. I was kind of dumb about some things.

After a long spell of present opening we'd hear the cat crying to come inside, so I'd open the door to some snow-covered object that stalked inside and gave us glances that could kill. We were soon forgiven though when the cat sniffed out a little package that smelled like catnip. He tore it open roughly, there being no ribbon to snip carefully, and tossed the catnip mouse around until finally breaking it open and eating most of the catnip. Whatever was left got vacuumed up on Christmas morning, just the first of many, many chores for that day.

By the way, in case you are wondering, the cat's name was Smudge. I don't know why, but my parents said I had once called him that, and the name stuck.

On Christmas Eve, after the orgy of the presents, we quickly put on our good clothes and got ready for church. I could wear my new sweater and shirt or whatever I had just unwrapped, but had to fold them carefully and put them on display under the tree when we came home.

Church began at 11 o'clock. (None of the midnight mass Catholic thing for us good Methodists.) I think my father slept through most of the service, since he'd been up from around 5 o'clock that morning. If he snored my mother poked him gently and he'd cry out in a loud voice, "What?" If the choir was singing it didn't matter, but sometimes the minister was preaching or giving his interminable prayer. I think there were some other snores in the church, too, and quite a few kids who rattled around in their seats while wishing they were home to see if Santa Claus was coming.

After church we sorted out our coats, hats, scarves and overshoes, all of which had been placed on chairs in the Ladies' Parlor behind the sanctuary. There were "Merry Christmases" all around, then we went outside to dust the new snow off the car. It always snowed on Christmas Eve. Otherwise it wouldn't have been fair to the kids who got new sleds.

And so to bed.

But not for long. At least the alarm rang early for my mom and dad. They had to get up and get the dinner started. First order of business was crumbling up the stale bread that had been left open to get even staler. With my dad working at a bakery, there was never a shortage of bread. Turkey giblets had to be cooked, the onions chopped and spices put into a huge bowl for mixing. When the turkey was stuffed—and what a monster it was—my dad took it to bake in the oven of the extra gas stove in the cellar.

Now came breakfast, often a big white or molasses sugar cookie and milk, with maybe a bowl of cereal, too. Forget nutrition, anything to get breakfast out of the way before the onslaught of relatives and almost relatives.

The day before Christmas I had hurled a big hubbard squash at the cellar floor time after time until it broke in pieces spewing seeds and gook everywhere. The main pieces were salvaged and cooked in a huge pot. I had to sweep up the seeds and gook.

For Christmas dinner potatoes had to be peeled, cans of cranberries opened and put like quivering lumps of jelly on plates. My mother and I had spent hours a couple of days before Christmas pulling the dining room table open as far as it would go and inserting leaves, putting on pads and a fancy table cloth. Goblets (for water, not wine) were taken out of the china cabinet and wiped until they sparkled. I was always mystified by the goblets because they shined with all the colors of the rainbow, and I liked to turn each one around and around to see the colors change.

The fancy dishes that were used only on Christmas were brought forth, as was the good silverware that usually needed to be polished before it could be used.

I had to prepare a relish tray of celery, carrot sticks, radishes, home made pickles (I ate one for every one I put on the dish), green onions, and olives. The olives suffered the same fate as the pickles.

Just when things seemed under control the guests began to arrive. Usually the first were the Walkers, Fred, Dora, and adult son, Harold, AKA Grease or Greasey. They had to come early, they thought, because Dora was bringing the cabbage salad. It was always a very good salad, too. Once I had to take something to her the day before Christmas and found her chopping away with a curved blade in a big wooden bowl held on her lap. The cabbage was chopped as fine as you could do now with a food processor, and there were tiny chunks of pineapple mixed in. The dressing was simply pineapple juice and mayonnaise.

Dora's husband, Fred, was a quiet man always in his 60s as much as I remember. He died while I was young, so I don't have a clear impression of him. He was delegated to tend the turkey in the cellar. I think he chose the job. That way he could get some time out from listening to Dora and Harold talk.

They didn't really talk to you, they yelled. Dora, who was always referred to by everyone else as Mother Walker, plunked herself at the kitchen table and harangued my mother, calling frequently for responses. My mother had no idea what Mother Walker was nattering on about, having her mind on the dinner.

In the living room Harold, called Grease by everyone except his parents (and me), cornered my father. He and Mother Walker always talked at full volume. When they were both in our small living room after dinner, both talked at once, trying to outshout each other. Grease had only three topics of conversation. First was his job (menial) at the Upson Co., which made paperboard called Upson board, and Tuco brand jigsaw puzzles. His second topic was the union he belonged to. You might have thought that Grease was the president, but if the truth were known I doubt if he ever attended a union meeting.

The third topic of conversation was circuses. Grease hardly ever went to one, even the little one that sometimes came to Lockport or the bigger Shrine Circus that played in Buffalo once a year. He got all of his information from *Billboard Magazine.*

What Mother Walker talked about I can't remember, but it must have been equally boring. Years later, when we finally got a telephone, she'd call my mother and talk for an hour or two. My mother gently placed the phone on the kitchen counter and went about her business, returning every now and then to say, "Yes, yes, that's right." When the line was dead Mother Walker had said goodbye and hung up. Maybe we didn't get a phone for many years because my mother had some sort of premonition of these calls.

Next to arrive for the Christmas feast, usually, were my father's uncle, Tonius, his aunt, Lilly Blosser and her husband, Art. Art was a big and blustery man who worked for the gas company as an installer. He probably had the muscles to prove it, but I never saw him in short sleeves, let alone topless. Always a suit with a tie. Aunt Lilly wouldn't have permitted him to wear anything that the Baptist church told her was unseemly. She was prim and proper, dignified, and quiet.

Tonius, who lived with them, tried to sneak into the background and take a nap. That was easy, Grease and Mother Walker did all the talking. However, each of them demanded some audience. Dora called out to my mother, "Florence, Florence," when my mother's attention seemed to wander. Grease shouted, "Frank, Frank, I say, I told Jim Upson, (owner of the Upson Co.) just the other day.... Blah, Blah, Blah." Grease had probably never exchanged two words with Upson, but the story went on at full volume.

Art Blosser interrupted every once in a while, loudly demanding, "Grease, I can't listen to you talk without a cigar." Grease reached into the vest pocket of his blue pin-striped suit and pulled forth cigars, passing them to Art, Tonius, and my dad. They all lit up, settled down and let Grease ramble on. I think everybody wished that he had been on the radio. Then they could have turned down the volume, maybe even shut him off for a while.

When Fred Walker ventured forth from the cellar where he had been basting the turkey, he looked askance at the smoking cigars. He never indulged. Grease usually didn't either when his father was around, but just passed them out to the others. When his dad wasn't there, Grease most often lit up a Pall Mall cigarette, but this was a holiday that deserved cigars. Cigarettes were sometimes Grease's fourth topic of conversation, but after proclaiming Pall Malls the best in creation, what more was there to say? Especially when everyone else was sort of nodding behind clouds of smoke.

I played under the Christmas tree with one of my new toys. Sometimes I could escape outside to play with Jimmy or Howard. Jack was at his grandmother's, and Doris and Audrey Donner were probably at some relative's, too.

There were still more relatives to come to our house, my grandmother, Uncle Butz and Aunt Bert from the country. Since my grandmother was blind and had lost a leg to diabetes, getting her into the side door and up the three steps to the first floor was a considerable task.

My mother went to help, I was sent to get the cat out of the way and my father policed the area to take away any cotton rugs that could trip up my grandmother's crutches. Butz and Bert steadied her along, and Dora and Grease yelled all the louder.

My grandmother was deaf as well as blind, so the Walkers had to pick up the volume so she could hear. As though she cared what either of them had to say, although my grandmother was alone so much that she was sometimes glad just to hear another voice. For a while. It was pretty easy to get tired of listening to Mother Walker and Grease.

I have no idea what Mother Walker's husband talked about, if he ever got a turn. I don't think he would interrupt anyone and so rarely got a chance to open his mouth.

Here we were then, my mother and father and me, Mother Walker, Fred Walker, Harold (Grease) Walker, Uncle Tonius, Uncle Art, Aunt Lilly, my grandmother, Aunt Bert and Uncle Butz. Quite a large crowd for our dining room, but we all fit somehow. Water goblets were filled, and sometimes there was even a little glass of cranberry juice before dinner. Wow, were we living it up for Christmas!

Mother Walker's salad was in a fancy bowl, the potatoes were mashed and keeping warm along with the gravy and squash on the back of the monster kitchen stove, and rolls, courtesy of Cousin Hugo's bakery, were in the warming oven. All that was lacking was the turkey. Fred Walker went to the cellar to retrieve it. The cat that had been swept aside when my grandmother arrived smelled the bird and came forth from somewhere just in time to get between Mr. Walker's legs as he carried the big hot roaster up the cellar stairs.

Down he went with a yell that even drowned out Dora and Harold for a moment. His glasses went flying, leaving him helpless. The turkey roaster crashed down with him, but luckily he didn't get burned by splashing grease. The turkey stayed in the roaster. Mostly. The cat, whose tail had been trodden on firmly, screeched and departed.

Everyone rushed to the scene, Dora and Harold turning up the volume, giving us all a play by play as though it had been a football game. Only my grandmother stayed in her chair, which was fortunate since her crutches would only have added to the chaos.

Mr. Walker's glasses were located, a bit bent but otherwise all right. He put them on, righted himself and the roaster, scooped up the turkey, which had suffered no damage, and marched up the stairs. The day had been saved.

We all stuffed ourselves at dinner with turkey, dressing, mashed potatoes, squash, cranberry jelly, cabbage salad, rolls and butter, the raw relishes, whatever pickles and olives I hadn't already eaten, and another cooked vegetable. All this ended with warm pie, mince and pumpkin, both homemade and both served with a generous chunk of very sharp and crumbly cheese. Almost everyone protested that they shouldn't eat any pie, then took a piece of each one.

Tea would be served later with homemade fruitcake if anyone could work up the appetite for it. Everyone not only could but did after an interval.

Next came a great clattering of dishes in the kitchen. Aunt Bert and Aunt Lilly cleared the table very efficiently, my mother washed the dishes, maybe leaving the fragile goblets for later, and my grandmother was plopped onto a kitchen chair and handed a towel so she could feel part of things by drying the dishes.

Mother Walker took another kitchen chair and continued to talk loud enough to be heard above the sounds of the work, as if anyone cared. In the living room Uncle Butz sat quietly and answered an occasional question about the farm from Uncle Art. Tonius dozed, and my father looked dazed as he tried to keep an eye on me, hear what Art and Butz were saying, and still make Grease think he was listening to him.

Once all the dishes had been washed, dried, and stacked back on the buffet so my mother and I could put them away the next day, it was time for the "sacrificial lamb." That was my Aunt Bert. She was packed off with Grease to whatever movie was playing downtown at the Palace Theater. She didn't want to go with Grease, of course, but in the interest of noise pollution control she went. Grease thought it was wonderful, his one date of the year. He'd even put his arm around Bert in the dark theater. Now Mother Walker had the floor to herself.

All too soon for us, but not for Bert, the movie ended, and she and Grease returned to the house, where my mother urged everyone to have a piece of fruitcake and cup of tea and maybe a turkey sandwich. Shortly after dark Uncle Butz announced that he had to go home and do the farm chores, which meant that Bert and my grandmother had to pack up and go, too.

Tonius soon had to tend the coal boiler at the school where he was the janitor. The boiler demanded attention no matter that it was Christmas and the school would remain closed for another week. Uncle Art proclaimed (over Grease's constant yelling) that he had to go home, tomorrow was a work day. Tonius roused himself, warmed up the car, and he and Art with Aunt Lilly in tow departed. Finally the Walkers left. Peace was restored. Blessed silence. There was no radio playing that night. The house was still vibrating from all the talking.

We all sat quietly for a while. My mother knitted, I played with a quiet new toy or read a new book—always a favorite present—and my dad just tried to get the noise out of his head. Before long we went to bed. Another Christmas had ended. It had been just like the one last year and the one before that and before that for as far back as I could remember. Except that the cat had created extra excitement that was a once-in-a-lifetime bonus.

My father got up early and went to deliver bread the next day, although he came home earlier than usual, saying, "The day after a holiday you might just as well not take the truck on the road. Nobody is buying food." My mother spent a good part of the day in her favorite rocking chair, after she had first turned its cushion upside down.

Uncle Art had sat there as usual and tipped way back, letting all of the coins slip quietly out of his pockets and under the cushion. I guess my mother thought the stray nickels, dimes, and quarters she collected were little enough reward for all she had been through the day before.

Chapter 5

ADVENTURES IN SHOPPING

Whenever my mother and dad bought something they liked to deal with small independent businesses. They didn't have many other choices if they shopped in Lockport. The only chain stores were Sears and Roebuck, which sold a few tools but mostly took catalogue orders, Montgomery Ward, which wasn't much bigger than the locally-owned stores, and the 5 and 10-cent stores on Main St.

I suppose my dad especially favored small businesses because he worked for one that was gradually getting smaller and smaller. It had probably been in decline since I was born, but there was no connection between the two events. It was just timing, but I think this confirmed his notions about doing business whenever possible with small local places.

The smallest of the business people my folks dealt with had no offices at all and worked from their homes. At least a couple times a year an antique little car chugged slowly to a halt in front of our house, and a tall man with a brief case got out. One of his legs was shorter than the other, and he wore one shoe with about a two-inch lift. He walked with a decided limp that didn't seem to interfere with his business. He was Walter B. Thayer, one of two insurance agents my folks had bought policies from. I don't know why they split their business between two agents. Maybe each one represented different companies or handled different lines, or maybe it was just to spread the money around.

I also never understood why Mr. Thayer had to come to the house twice a year. I doubt if my folks were continually taking out new policies. It could have been renewals, premiums to be paid, or Mr. Thayer just wanted to keep them up to date on whatever changes in insurance coverage had been made by his company. I'm not even sure if it was life insurance or something to do with the car or house that brought him to see us.

Mr. Thayer and my dad sat in the living room, and the talk began, ever so slowly. Insurance was never mentioned, but we all knew that's where the conversation would wind up eventually. First there was talk about church, then what was going on at the bakery, news about some of Mr. Thayer's other clients that my folks knew. Maybe this last topic was to prove that, contrary to what they might have thought, Mr. Thayer really did have other clients. All this might be followed by a general discussion of local and national news.

My father's eyelids got heavier and heavier. He had gotten up at 5 o'clock and wanted to get to bed. But Mr. Thayer talked on and on. Eventually the talk turned to insurance but even then wandered along a leisurely course toward the real business at hand. I had long since departed for the kitchen to do homework, read a book, torment the cat and have a snack. If things continued long enough I went through the living room and departed up the stairs for bed.

After a few hours Mr Thayer put on his hat and coat, maneuvered slowly down the sidewalk to his old car and chugged off into the night. Exactly what had been accomplished I was never sure.

Apparently selling insurance didn't fill all of Mr. Thayer's time. He also made ornate lighted outdoor Christmas ornaments. He displayed one on his own porch, which wasn't far from our house, but I never saw another anywhere in Lockport. A high-pressure salesman he wasn't, but his competitor for our business, if they could even be called competitors, was even less energetic.

Once in a while we got a phone call, and whoever answered it heard, "This is Henry Brum, Brum, Brum, Brumley. Is Frank Senior. th, th, th, there?" It was indeed Henry Brumley who was threatening an appearance at our door within minutes. He lived almost directly behind our house, across Pine Street, so could drive around the corner in two minutes. He could have walked almost as fast, but big, important businessmen didn't walk to their appointments.

He was soon at the door, always looking the same, a roly-poly little man dressed in a brown suit with a vest and brown tie. He had on a brown overcoat and derby hat. He and my folks sat in the living room and again the talk ranged over everything except insurance. Whatever Mr. Brumley said took considerable time because of his stutter. I'd leave the living room even faster than when Mr. Thayer came to call. From the kitchen I could hear Mr. Brumley try, try, try, trying to say some, some, something and I wanted to shout, "Spit it out Henry." Of course, I never did.

I think all of the stuttering eventually led dad to buy or renew whatever policy Henry was trying to sell. It probably could have been done by mail and if so a whole lot faster, but that wasn't how things were done in our house. Why those two particular agents? Maybe some sort of equal opportunity program.

Buying a new car had that same aura of "professionalism." Our car had come from Mullane Motors, Lockport's Plymouth dealer, and was always taken back there for whatever repairs were needed. Mullane Motors was tucked away on a side street near the canal and had an expansive showroom that was probably big enough to hold one or maybe even two cars if they weren't big station wagons. The used car lot was also tiny and the repair shop was about gas station size.

The star—maybe only—salesman was Howard Fritz. His son, Merle, and I were in Scouts together. My dad and Mr. Fritz came to Scout functions whenever dads were wanted to drive the troop somewhere. During the general "talking time" that took place after church every Sunday I expect Howard sometimes danced around the idea of us buying a new car but got no encouragement. Then came the war, and there were no new cars available. After the war when new Plymouths could be obtained and I had safely mastered driving, Mr. Fritz said it was finally time to retire the 1936. He said he'd drive a new 1948 model over to our house some evening so we could look it over, and that's exactly what he did.

My mother, dad and I piled in with Mr. Fritz for a test drive. Mr. Fritz explained the new features. The speedometer, instead of being dinner plate size as it was in the '36, was much smaller. This left room on the control panel for a radio (to be installed at extra cost if wanted.) The old 1936 model had never had one, of course. The gearshift of the new Plymouth was now on the steering column, and the choke and throttle knobs were gone and apparently no longer needed to get thunder from the engine. There was a handle to control turn signals. No need for the driver to fling his arm out the window any more to indicate a turn.

The starter pedal was gone. Now you just turned the key to fire up the engine. Marvelous bits of progress, every one of them. Soon my mother and dad and Mr. Fritz were poring over color samples and after delivering us back home Mr. Fritz departed with a signed purchase order. He didn't get a check. My folks didn't have a checking account. There was a bank account for savings and annual payments like taxes, but other purchases were all in cash.

Mr. Fritz arranged a loan of some kind and got the license plates transferred. On the appointed day he delivered the car to our house, some papers were signed, the license plates were switched, and he drove away in the old 1936 Plymouth. We never saw it again.

Mr. Fritz's wife, Ida, loved flowers and went with Howard if he was going to call on a customer who had a great garden. At one point she decided that the City of Lockport should have more flowers, especially in little grassy triangles where some streets met. She took it upon herself to dig flowerbeds and plant them at half a dozen places in Lockport. She watered diligently, pulled weeds and tended them the way she did at home. At age 90 she was still at it, but by that time some garden clubs had come to her assistance and had even put up at least one bronze plaque in one of the gardens in her honor. Lockport appreciated enterprise.

Most of the other things my family bought came from little Lockport stores. In addition to the two small locally-owned department stores, there were a couple of men's shops, Carnahan & Shearer and Lerch & Daly. They frequently came up short on having the proper sizes and any selection of colors, so we made an occasional grand shopping expedition to Buffalo.

This was no idle venture. It took at least a week of planning and checking the paper and radio for weather forecasts. Somehow my dad could cover the bakery route faster than usual on days when he wanted to go somewhere. It was usually on a Saturday.

As soon as he got home after lunch we'd start off on the 30-mile-or-so trek to Buffalo. We didn't go downtown, but out to the east side to the Broadway-Filmore shopping district. Apparently everybody in Buffalo and the surrounding area had chosen the same day to come. We had never seen such crowds, but after circling around several blocks a parking space opened up.

The big drawing card in the neighborhood was the huge Sattler's department store, 998 Broadway, as its radio ads always said. Prices were cheap, cheap, cheap. Quality was about the same, but for some things that didn't matter much. Crowds pushed up and down the aisles, and my father looked totally dazed.

Sattler's couldn't be ignored on any shopping trip, but the real target of our excursion was next door at Posmantur's men's wear, a narrow store several stories high. Here salesmanship was polished to a high art. We were greeted at the front door by a suave and friendly gent who wanted to know what department we wanted.

My mother indicated that we wanted to buy a suit for me. "Fifth floor," said the greeter, leading us to the elevator and giving the operator specific directions, "fifth floor, no other stops." There wasn't anyone else on the elevator nor anyone waiting to go up to any other floor, so it didn't matter, but we had to get "special treatment."

As we left the elevator on the fifth floor we were seized by another greeter and turned over to a salesman who was more unctuous than Uriah Heep. He whipped out his tape measure or measured by eye and led us to a rack of suits. He pulled a coat out of the bunch and jammed me into it. The sleeves were too short. He tugged them down, but it didn't help. Talking all the time about what wonderful merchandise he had, he put that coat back on a hanger and whipped out another and shoved me into it. Better, too big in the shoulders and flapping in the back, but he said that didn't matter because the tailor would take care of all of those little details.

Then he began pulling out suit after suit of the same size in different colors and fabrics. Prices he wouldn't talk about, but asked my mother all about living in Lockport and whether the canal was still there because he had been there once and seen it. He found out my father worked for a bakery. Strange coincidence, his own uncle had once owned a bakery. Chatter, chatter, chatter without let up while at the same time steering us toward one particular suit he wanted to unload on the country bumpkins.

Soon the tailor was there, and I had to put on the pants as well as the coat. The pants were a mile too long, but the tailor pinned them up and marked the cuffs. The seat was too big, but would be taken in. The coat needed this and that. The salesman grabbed the back in a great wad so I could see in the mirror how nice it would fit in front. Then he gathered up the front and smoothed the back. "The fit is wonderful," he lied, but my mother heard a popping noise, like a thread breaking. "A stitch broke in the seam in the back," she said. "Oh, the tailor will fix that without any problem," the salesman said and swept along toward the sale. I could feel an x being marked on my back. Fabric was stretched this way and that. It was a wonder that all the stitches didn't break.

The tailor pulled the collar up around my ears and at the same time tugged the bottom of the coat down as hard as he could, commenting, "Perfect, perfect." all the while and making hash marks with his chalk. The sleeves were too short so he tried to jerk them down hard. I thought my shoulder bone was going to go with each one as he pulled.

None of us knew what was going on, it was all so fast, but apparently somebody had already decided that we wanted the suit. I never said that and didn't hear my mother or father say any such thing. I didn't even think I liked the suit all that much, but this was no time to dally about making a decision. This was like a cavalry charge in the Saturday afternoon movies at the Rialto Theater.

On we sped, whether we knew where we were going or not. The salesman knew. The tailor wielded his tape measure, pins, and chalk at breakneck speed, like a surgeon who had done the same operation a hundred times. Both kept chattering, either to each other or to us, the victims. It was interesting how sales people at Posmantur's always knew exactly what the customers needed and how much money they had in their wallets. If my father had looked dazed in Sattler's, you should have seen him now.

By this time the salesman was on a first-name basis with all of us and had remembered that on his last visit to Lockport the lights seemed to blink. "What is it about lights in Lockport?" he asked. "They flicker all the time."

My father explained that the Lockport Light, Heat and Power Co. produced a different kind of power than was used in Buffalo and most other places. Lockport had 25 cycle current as opposed to 60 cycle in Buffalo. The 25 cycles were slower, and so the lights flickered. Living there, we never noticed it, but people from out of town always did and made remarks. Whenever we bought a radio and other small appliances we had to have it converted to work on 25 cycle current.

I'm sure the salesman was a scholar of electricity. He wanted to know all the details of the electrical system. Then he asked what kind of car we had come in. "It's such a long way from Lockport. Did you pack a lunch to eat on the way?" he asked. There was constant chatter and continual yanking at the suit trying to make it fit me.

After all the tugging was finished and the tailor's chalk marks had piled up like snow, the salesman flustered around writing on multiple tags and bills, putting our names and addresses on this line and that. At last the suit was whisked away to the tailor shop and we were gathered up and ushered grandly to the cashier where my father anted up the cash.

By now it was all so jolly that the salesman risked what he hoped would be taken as a joke. "Watch out, Frank," he said as my father opened his wallet, "don't let those moths out of there." My father made no response. He was never very free with money and knew it. How did that salesman know it?

We weren't done yet, however. No one ever escaped from Posmantur's that easily. We were swept along to another counter. We had to buy a shirt and tie to go with such a grand suit, the salesman said, and there ought to be another pair of pants to keep the suit pants nice. Maybe a sweater, too. My mother drew the line at that. Any sweaters that were needed she'd knit herself. The salesman retreated and quickly shifted to a discussion of the special socks, ties, underwear, pajamas that were all on sale. They were so cheap it would be almost like stealing them.

A nice overcoat and hat would dress up the suit and make me look like a movie star. He whipped a few coats from the rack, never bothering to look for the right size. He jammed me into one despite the fact that the sleeves were so tight I couldn't move my arms. "This is just for the feel of the material," he said, stripping the coat back off and almost instantly pouring me into one more or less the right size. "Maybe a coat with a fur collar," he said, "and how about a scarf? It gets very cold in Lockport, I understand."

I don't know how we escaped without buying anything more, but somehow we did. Finally we pushed our way to the elevator, and the salesman stayed right with us, holding my father's arm and talking all the way. When the elevator arrived my dad, mother, and I squeezed in and fled. Back on the first floor we were grabbed again by the greeter, who enquired if we had gotten everything we wanted and had we noticed the nice umbrellas right there by the front door. Did my father want a suit? Third floor and he started marching us back to the elevator.

We all rebelled at once and pushed our way to the street. My new suit would come in the mail so we wouldn't have to come back to Posmantur's for a year. My father's dazed look slowly faded. He'd loved every minute of it, being pushed and pulled, the clothes being forced on him and me, the tailor doing his little dance. It was better entertainment than listening to the radio or Grease Walker's monologues.

The next stop was the Broadway Market across the street. This was a vast collection of open-front stalls side by side all down a long building. Every stall sold something different and each, apparently, was individually operated. As soon as we got near the first stall the storekeeper reached out and nearly dragged us in. "Try this orange juice, I squeeze the oranges myself. Try it, try it." He forced a little paper cup on each of us. It was good, but we kind of drifted away as we drank it, and he didn't chase after us.

At the next stall it was the same routine with a sausage, the next had cheese, one had apples, another cider, yet another fresh horseradish that made our eyes run just from coming near it. We were tugged along from place to place and batted around like three tennis balls. My father thought it was wonderful, being so sought after. He tried to discuss what he wanted and didn't want, but the vendors weren't interested in talking. Some could barely speak English anyway and were more at home with Polish. After all, we were in a Polish section of Buffalo.

We ended up buying a little of the fresh horseradish because there was no place else we knew of that had it. And then some cheese and cold cuts. Despite the fact that my father got as much free bread as we could eat, we also somehow managed to acquire a long loaf of rye bread. We were so confused by it all that we didn't know what we had until we got home and opened the packages.

At length we also escaped from the "grabbers" at the market, found the car, and headed home. There was one last stop, Freddie's Donuts, a big glass and chrome paradise on Main Street in Buffalo that sold nothing but donuts, thousands of them. It had a door that opened by itself when we turned to leave the store while balancing a great pile of boxes. Lockport had nothing like the donut store or its magic door.

Wow, what a trip! We'd talk about it for weeks. We wondered if the suit was such a good buy. "Did you see the color in the daylight?" my mother asked. We hadn't. "Do you suppose the blue is too bright?" No one knew, but we hoped for the best. In a few days it arrived. It fit. Mostly. Anyway, I would grow out of it in a year or two.

There were also other kinds of excursions to Buffalo. There was a great movie theater unmatched by anything in Lockport, and the W. T. Grant store was better than any ten cent store at home. Once in a while we went to the zoo and almost every fall to see the chrysanthemums in the conservatory. Occasionally we took in an indoor circus. Each trip was separate. Rarely would we do two things together.

Getting to the circus, of course, was a huge undertaking, with arranging for tickets in advance and planning the bread route so that we'd be ready to go early in the afternoon.

The visit to the movie was usually a Sunday afternoon affair, also planned in advance, but only as early as we could see the movie ads in the Buffalo Sunday *Courier-Express*, our weekly look at the doings of the world outside Lockport.

Shea's Buffalo Theater on Main Street was a movie palace typical of those built in the 1920's. It had a large, ornate auditorium, with its walls thickly encrusted with gilded cherubs, curly cues, and borders. The seats were spacious and plush, not like those at the Rialto or even the Palace in Lockport. This was real luxury. Wonder of wonders, an organ rose from the floor with an organist already seated on the bench and playing. The theater trembled as the sound swelled.

"Rudolpho Charbonneauski (or something) at the Mighty Wurlitzer," intoned a Great Voice from the sky. A spotlight illuminated Rudolpho, who as far as we could see was dressed in a tuxedo. I knew what a tuxedo was. People wore them in movies if they didn't ride horses. Rudolpho threw a toothy smile at all of us over his shoulder and continued to bring what we considered to be great music from the Mighty Wurlitzer. (Wurlitzer had a factory somewhere near Buffalo, so there may have been some local pride in announcing the brand of organ.) I doubt if Rudolpho played any music by Bach, Rheinberger, Mendelssohn or any other of the classical composers who wrote for the organ. I wouldn't have known their names anyway. What we probably heard were themes from movies that had already played at the Shea's Buffalo theater, but it was magical.

After lifting our spirits high into the heavens, the organist and his instrument slowly settled back into the floor and out of sight. The spotlight on him faded, and the house lights slowly dimmed, leaving only the great illuminated maroon curtain across the stage. Then the curtain with its heavy gold fringe swept open silently to reveal a movie screen even bigger than the one at the Palace in Lockport.

With a final flourish from somewhere we couldn't see, Rudolpho struck his last notes, which were replaced in our ears soon by the sonorous tones of Lowell Thomas narrating a newsreel. The fantasy had to take time out for a dash of reality—a dust bowl and bread lines in America, a war threatening to break out in Europe, and unrest in other places. The audience could only stand so much tragedy, though. Mr. Thomas always found a bathing suit contest somewhere to show us.

After Lowell Thomas said goodbye, the great movie lion roared, and we were transported again into the land of make-believe where everything was elegant. The ladies wore long flowing gowns, the men were suave, and everybody lived in a Manhattan penthouse. It was many years later that I actually got to Manhattan and found that hardly anyone really lived in a penthouse. At least nobody I ever met.

After two hours of bliss in the darkened Shea's Buffalo world of fantasy, the house lights came back on, and the heavy velvet curtain closed over the screen. We made our way slowly to the street to find that gritty Buffalo was still there and the sunshine of Hollywood had been replaced by the cold gray weather of western New York State. There wasn't anyone wearing a tuxedo or long gown in sight. There was nothing to do but seek out the car and head for home.

Sometimes I guess my folks wanted to prolong the magic, so we went to a place they called Weesee's (it rhymed with Greasy's), but I had no idea of how the name was spelled. Weesee's was a neighborhood bar somewhere on Buffalo's east side. It didn't look like a bar but was a big gray house on a corner. One side of the building had a long enclosed sun porch, which was a kind of dining room, although Weesee's, as far as I knew, sold no meals except sandwiches. We always sat and froze on the unheated porch because that was the only part of the bar where kids were allowed.

There were only two things on Weesee's menu that we considered having. One was a ham and cheese sandwich, the other was limburger cheese. We always had the ham and cheese. The rye bread was sliced very, very thin, and the ham and Swiss cheese were also slivered into delicate slices and covered with the best mustard I had ever eaten. With the sandwich came a big piece of dill pickle. We never chose the limburger, but my mother often bought a block of limburger at the butcher's and we had limburger and onion sandwiches at home. It was a favorite supper when Tonius, Uncle Art and Aunt Lilly came. But we could only eat limburger and onions if Aunt Lilly wasn't going to one of her church meetings.

With Weesee's sandwiches we each had a big glass of root beer. I don't think it came out of a bottle but from a barrel and was something special, available only at Weesee's.

The sandwiches and root beer were delicious, but after freezing on Weesee's porch for a while we were ready to get in the car and turn on the heater. We might stop at Freddie's Donuts, but my dad had already spent a ton of money, so we might not bother with Mr. Freddy on this trip.

Chapter 6

THE BREAD OF LIFE-HUGO STYLE

Y ou've already encountered
some mention of my father's job at the Niagara Baking Co.,
but we generally called it Cousin Hugo's bakery. The boss'
name wasn't really Hugo. It wasn't even pronounced the way
most people would have said it, but HOO-go. He wasn't our
cousin either, and he didn't own the bakery, at least not all of
it, but it was an inviting place for me to visit. I was always
welcomed, and it had the most wonderful smells of fresh
bread, sweet rolls, and other goodies.

My father's uncle, Frank M. Bredell, started the bakery
before I was born. He must have had partners because Great
Uncle Frank wasn't the president but the secretary and treasurer of the bakery. I didn't care who owned the place, I just
thought it was fun to go there. As a matter of fact, in the years
I remember, Cousin Hugo, whose real name was Jonathan

Pfrang, ran the place, as much as anyone really ran it. The power behind the throne was Allen Van de Mark, who had been a mayor of Lockport and was a general big wheel in town. I don't know how Pfrang became Cousin Hugo. Probably the name was one my father gave him, just as he named Tonius and Grease Walker. Anyway, Cousin Hugo it was.

When the bakery was in its prime it had several deliverymen all of whom drove horses and wagons around town to peddle their goods. My father had driven a horse, too, but I think the horse was gone before I was born, or least before I could remember anything. What I recall is an old-fashioned white truck and later a long GMC truck painted orange. Why orange? Probably because it came that way and Cousin Hugo was too cheap to have it repainted. He did have the bakery's name lettered on the sides.

My dad finished his route in the early afternoon and drove the truck home and parked it in the street while he did some chores around the house. I guess he didn't want to go back to the bakery too early or someone would think he wasn't working, so he'd return later. Meanwhile, while the truck was parked, Jimmy Garlock and I turned it into a playroom. We did all kinds of make believe stuff in the back of it, then sat up front and "drove." That meant that I pressed the starter pedal on the floor while the truck was in gear and made it leap ahead. The engine didn't start, since we didn't have a key, but nevertheless there was a great noise, which always brought my father from the house to chase us out of the truck.

Sometimes he took me to the bakery with him, I suppose just to get me out of my mother's hair for a while, but I never realized that. It was a treat for me. The bakery had two locations, a store on West Main Street and the bread bakery on State Road. The store was best. That was where the cakes and cookies were made, and there were always free samples to be had from Blanche, who was clerk, cashier and "little mother" to everyone who worked at the bakery, especially Hugo himself. She could have had a full-time job just keeping him on track and making sure he got things done. He was disorganization personified.

Every Christmas Eve, about four in the afternoon, Hugo should have been busy getting out the special orders for cakes and the turkeys and hams that had been roasted for the lodges or clubs that were planning Christmas Eve dinners.

Instead he raced around the store, accomplishing nothing, then suddenly shouted out, "Cripes, it's Christmas Eve, and I haven't got nothing done yet," meaning that he hadn't bought his wife a Christmas present and hadn't even thought about what to buy. By then the major stores were closing for the holiday. Most people had finished their shopping and even wrapping. Not Hugo.

He ran around the bakery a little more, stirring up dust. (There is always flour dust to be stirred up in a bakery, if no other kind, and if the truth were told there was the regular dust kind of dust there, too.) But Hugo never paid any attention to dust of any sort. Soon he raced across Main Street to Bob Grimble's store which sold mostly hardware, hunting and fishing equipment and licenses, as well as a few small home appliances and tiny radios.

What Hugo got his wife for Christmas from that array is anyone's guess. The only other nearby place that was still open was the liquor store next door to the bakery. That's where he usually did his shopping. If his wife didn't fancy her present, Hugo could always drink it himself.

Hugo liked a bit of the bottle and always gave an employee party every summer on his yacht. Calling the boat a yacht may be giving it too grand a name, but the little vessel was tied up in a dock at Olcott Beach and never ventured into Lake Ontario. Running the engine would have cost money, and Hugo didn't want to spend any, so the boat stayed idle. That was just as well, too. The only activity at the party—a stag affair to which not even Blanche was invited— was drinking beer. My father went unwillingly to these binges but never enjoyed them. He didn't much care for the taste of beer and didn't fancy watching anyone get so drunk they'd fall over the boat railing into the skuzzy harbor water, which at least one person did every year. Fortunately the Coast Guard never had to be called.

Hugo was always friendly when I went to the bakery but was in the utmost panic so didn't say much more than "Hello, I've got to get out of here. Cripes, I was due at the dentist at 2:30, and now it's quarter to four. Cripes." And away he'd go in a great flurry.

Blanche had more time for me. There weren't usually many customers, and even if there were she'd invite me to help myself to the cookies spread out on great pans. Hugo's cookies weren't like the neatly packaged ones you find in stores now. They were large and the next best thing to homemade.

Cookies and sweet rolls weren't wrapped but were counted out into a white paper bag for each customer. Sliced white and whole wheat bread were wrapped by machine, but rye and pumpernickel were sold in open-end paper bags. They may not have looked like much, but Hugo's breads tasted good and weren't like the sponge rubber that is now called bread in America. It had a little toughness to it, body, texture and flavor. Remember when bread had flavor? Maybe not, if you are still on the sunny side of 50.

Every afternoon after finishing his route my father had to go into the store and "settle up." That meant he had to count the money he had taken in. Nobody paid by check. Then Blanche counted it. If they didn't agree they had to do it again until they did. Then my dad would have to count the unsold bread and the day-old bread he'd taken back from the stores for credit.

These credits were subtracted from what he "owed" for what he had taken out, and if all went well, the totals came out right. When they didn't he and Blanche would have to refigure until it all worked out. They certainly didn't want me in the way during all this, so they sat me down at the antique mechanical typewriter and let me bang away. When I took typing in high school we had some pretty old typewriters but nothing nearly as old as the one at the bakery. I hammered the keys, getting big wads of them stuck together. It didn't seem to matter because the typewriter wasn't used for much of anything else anyway. All orders and bills were hand-written.

Out in the back room, where the cakes and cookies were baked, was a guy named Al, all dusty with flour. He was always dressed in white from his little round cloth hat to his white shirt, pants and shoes. It sounds wonderfully clean, but it wasn't. There apparently was no way that the wooden floors and tables could be kept spotless, so things went on as they went. The state and city health inspectors weren't always pleased when they visited the bakery and often threatened to shut it down, but they never did.

Anyway, Blanche and Al finally got married, and then Al learned that he was allergic to flour. What an affliction for a baker.

While the sweets were baked behind the store, bread was made at the bakery located a few blocks away on State Road. It had no sign on it, which was just as well since it looked more like a barn than anything else. The outside walls hadn't been painted in years and were rough, weather-beaten boards. The inside didn't look any better. Flour was moved around in big wooden wagons that resembled overgrown laundry carts. They didn't look like they could be washed or ever had been.

The mixing machine was huge and had big arms that pummeled the dough, but there didn't seem to be any way to get inside to clean that either, so it just accumulated little bits of dough year by year. The wooden floors were littered with tiny crusts of rye bread, the little pointed ends that were cut off and discarded because the loaves couldn't be wrapped if they were shaped like bullets with rounded ends. As a matter of fact, they weren't really wrapped. They were tied together with string and put into paper bags. The little crusts were supposed to end up in wooden barrels. Some of them did, but the barrels often overflowed all over the floor. Every time I visited the bakery I did my bit to control the situation by eating a few of the newer crusts from the barrels.

Wrapped bread was stacked on steel racks which the drivers (my dad and only one other man when the bakery was nearing the end of its existence) could wheel onto the bakery porch to be loaded into their trucks. The only way to get the racks outside was through a large sliding door, the kind that farmers have on their barns. Every time this vast door opened some of the bakers yelled very loudly from inside the bakery, "Shut that door." Apparently cold air interfered with the rising of the dough, but no one ever thought of putting in a different kind of entry.

My dad took me on the route with him sometimes, especially if he wanted to get finished early so we could go somewhere. I failed to see how I could help him get finished faster, since I really had very little grasp of which bread was which. He'd go into a restaurant kitchen and tell me to bring six white, two pullman (long sandwich loaves), three rye and a whole wheat. I'd try to remember all of that and probably get it mixed up and take in the wrong amounts. Then I'd have to go back out, and he'd usually go out, too, to get me straightened out once again. Any time saving must have been minimal.

I got inside places I otherwise wouldn't have seen and never hope to see again—the jail, the county poorhouse and an orphanage. At the jail the trusties did the cooking and seemed more like employees than prisoners. They apparently had the run of the kitchen. My dad said they wouldn't try to escape. They had no place to go and managed to get into trouble deliberately every fall to get a warm place to spend the winter.

At the county poorhouse a bunch of old men also did the cooking, old guys with no teeth who drooled as they put away the bread. Sometimes they offered me one of their homemade cookies or something (as though there weren't plenty of cookies at the bakery). After seeing the drooling and their runny noses I declined the cookies.

Sometimes on Saturdays my dad had to deliver cakes to halls for wedding receptions. Hugo's people weren't too prompt getting the cakes decorated so often the wedding reception was already under way when my dad arrived.

Almost always he was invited to dance with the bride and have a drink of homemade wine. He might dance but tried to avoid the wine. Lockport was the kind of place where deliverymen were invited to share in the parties, at least in what we now (not then) call "ethnic" neighborhoods. These quaint customs didn't apply at the uppity Tuscarora Club or the country club. No member there would even *think* of dancing with the hired help or a bread man.

Chapter 7

UNDAUNTED BY DEPRESSION, EVEN LOCKPORT WENT TO WAR

In the late 1930s the clouds of war were gathering. Even the undernourished little Lockport newspaper, the *Union-Sun & Journal*, let its readers know that there was something unfortunate going on in Europe. Of course the war news had to take a back seat to the doings of the ladies league of the Evangelical Church and the potluck dinners at the Methodist Church, but still, careful readers could get the notion that there was trouble afoot. Some of the more perspicacious might even have foreseen that the United States would get involved eventually.

Without Lockport's help, Franklin D. Roosevelt got elected to the White House in 1932, and the country was ready for his New Deal. I was too young to know anything about it, of course, but in the bastion of Republicanism, Lockport was happy with the depression of Herbert Hoover. Times might have been bad, but at least the man in the White House was "one of ours." There were no unemployment checks for those not working, and jobs were scarce, but all the same he was the kind of a man Lockport knew and loved—a Republican. When FDR ran against Herbert Hoover for president in 1932 and offered the prospect of a New Deal, Lockport staunchly faced the rear and voted for Hoover by a margin of 3-2.

Fortunately, my dad was never without work during the Great Depression that lasted through most of the 1930s. The Niagara Baking Co. continued to operate, and people still bought bread and even some sweet rolls, eclairs, etc. I didn't know we were in a depression, and I don't remember seeing signs of it in Lockport, other than the unemployed men who would come to the door begging food. If there was a Hooverville, a city of shacks for the jobless and homeless, it was well out of sight. The *Union-Sun & Journal* certainly never printed anything about such abominations.

I still had 10 cents a week to go to the Rialto Theater on Saturdays. During the newsreel everyone booed Franklin Roosevelt loudly. Being as dumb as I was, I joined in. Once I even went to school wearing a Landon for President campaign button. That must have been in 1936, when Alf Landon, the bland governor of Kansas, was the Republican nominee for president. Some kid who must have been a Democrat threatened to beat me up because of the pin, so I took it off. I didn't know anything about politics anyway.

Roosevelt ignored Landon, and so did the country, giving Roosevelt the greatest reelection turnout of any president in history. Nevertheless, Lockport went for Landon by almost the same margin that it had given Hoover four years earlier.

There were lots of Roosevelt haters in Lockport during his long tenure in office and for years later. The locals conveniently overlooked the fruits of the Roosevelt years—the jobs created for the unemployed; the political and economic advance of blacks (Lockport wouldn't have been much concerned about that in any case); farm price supports; introduction of electricity and the resulting industry in large parts of the country; a large array of public works projects from new parks to roads, bridges and college dormitories; stabilization of the banks that had gone broke under Hoover; securities regulation; Social Security; child labor and minimum wage laws; and the end of the depression without letting the country drift into communism.

Lockport accepted the fruits of the New Deal but never supported it. When the Republicans put up Wendell Wilkie in 1940 he got the biggest vote in Lockport any Republican had during Roosevelt's long time in office. He got swamped nationally, but if the nation had followed Lockport's example he would have won by the same 3-2 margin.

In 1944, when New York's Republican governor, Thomas E. Dewey, thought he could move into the White House, he carried Lockport by nearly the same margin. The Lockport Republicans never gave up.

My mother, dad, and I were at home the afternoon of Sunday, December 7, 1941. Blossers and Tonius were visiting, and everybody was in an after-dinner stupor half discussing plans for the upcoming Christmas. (What had to be discussed? Every year it was the same thing.)

The radio was muttering quietly in the background, and it was possible to hear it, the Walkers not being present. Suddenly there was a news bulletin:

"President Roosevelt said in a statement today that the Japanese had attacked Pearl Harbor, Hawaii, from the air."

This was followed by a second bulletin about an attack on Manila in the Philippines During the attack in Hawaii half of the American naval fleet was destroyed. The air force was left with only 16 serviceable bombers.

The next day the president called a joint session of Congress during which he gave his report about the attack, calling December 7 "a date which shall live in infamy." The United States was at war with Japan and within three days against Germany and Italy as well.

Some people blamed Roosevelt for letting this happen, but Lockport went to war with the rest of the country. The previous October America had starting drafting young men into the army, and as the war intensified more and more homes in Lockport sported little flags that had a blue star in the center of a red and white background. It meant someone was in military service. In late 1942, when I started delivering newspapers, I noticed that many of the blue stars had been replaced by gold. A death in service.

I was only 11 when war broke out and 15 when it ended,

so I escaped the draft, but knew some of the young men who were called. Our scoutmaster was one. After he was released from service he returned a changed man. He wasn't fun any more. Probably had had too much discipline in the army and maybe had seen and done things he wanted to try to forget.

A huge effort was initiated in Washington and spread into every city, village and crossroads of the country to make every American feel that this was *our* war even though we were an ocean away from any battlefield. The propaganda war was waged as fiercely as the shooting war. "Win the war" slogans and posters were everywhere. Women replaced men in factories, and songs like *Rosie the Riveter* were popular.

Servants, store clerks, waitresses, doormen, messengers, etc. abandoned their regular jobs and flocked to war plants, where they not only earned more money but basked in the idea that they were part of the war effort.

Hollywood went to war, turning out pictures that glamorized the military, and popular songs that degraded Japan and Germany were everywhere. I still went to the Rialto every Saturday afternoon, taking in the newsreel that always reported American victories, even when we were losing the war.

There were such pictures as *Guadalcanal Diary*, *The Purple Heart*, *Bataan*, *See Here Private Hargrove*, *30 Seconds Over Tokyo* and a long list of others that were mostly forgettable. They weren't all serious. *Four Jills in a Jeep* set out to prove that war can be fun. When they weren't making movies, actors made pictures for the War Department to boost morale and make sure everyone was attuned to the war effort. Actors also entertained at military bases around the world and led the campaigns to sell war bonds.

In California Japanese-Americans were rounded up and imprisoned in camps on the premise that they might side with Japan, even though most of them had been born in this country.

In four years the national debt skyrocketed from 48 billion dollars to 247 billion. Americans paid higher taxes but also invested in 6 billion dollars of war bonds.

The effort to sell war bonds reached far down, even into my sixth grade class. We didn't have $18.75 to buy a bond, which would be worth $25 if we kept it 10 years. But we did have some nickels and dimes we could lend the government. We bought savings stamps and pasted them in little books. When we had bought $18.75 worth of stamps we could trade the book in for a bond. The stamps paid no interest, but we didn't care about that. We just wanted to buy more and more of them to help win the war. Every teacher sold the war stamps, and there was a regular time each week when we would buy them and report how many we had. I suppose the oral report was a way of shaming any slackers to buy more. As I said, the propaganda effort was fierce.

Part of the propaganda urged us to "do without." We were encouraged to get along with less because many goods were rationed and others were just unobtainable. Whenever we wanted to buy something, like Christmas lights, that were in short supply, the store clerk would always say, "Don't ya know there's a war on?" Many simple things disappeared from the shelves, such as hairpins and alarm clocks (the steel was needed for guns, they told us). The last car rolled down the assembly line February 10, 1942, and the machinery then was converted to make war equipment. Things made of steel went off the market. I had taught myself to type and wanted to buy a portable typewriter. There wasn't a used or new one anywhere to be found until the war was over. I still have that Smith Corona portable I bought when the first ones came back on the market.

Tissues such as Kleenex were scarce. Maybe the paper that would have been used to make them was used to print war propaganda. Toilet paper was also sometimes scarce but never disappeared entirely. Cigarettes were often unavailable, and people tried to roll their own. The War Production Board had great power over the economy and sharply restricted the construction of new houses. Building materials were needed to build and expand military bases.

Everyone had ration books from which little stamps were torn out to buy things—red stamps for meat, blue stamps for processed food, other colors for gasoline and clothing. Every week on page one of the Lockport *Union-Sun and Journal* there was a review of what the ration allotments were for that week.

Among the other rationed goods were butter, sugar, coffee, canned and frozen foods, shoes, and most clothing. Men's pants went cuffless, vests and double-breasted jackets and some pockets were banned, all in the guise that the saving of material would somehow clothe a soldier.

Women's bathing suits got skimpier, promoting the widespread use of the formerly rare two-piece suit. I'm not sure how the change in bathing suits was supposed to clothe a soldier, but I suppose the GIs appreciated the new pin-up pictures of bathing beauties.

Old toothpaste tubes had to be turned in to buy new ones. (They were made of metal in those days, not plastic.)

Our boy scout troop went door to door collecting newspapers and empty tin cans, which were sold at the junkyard and recycled. Kitchen grease was saved in a tin can and turned in at the butcher shop.

Manufacturers vied with each other to put forth the best and biggest claims about how they were helping the war effort. Auto companies, striving to keep their brand names alive, prattled on about their production of airplanes and tanks.

Lucky Strike cigarettes carried its part of the war effort to new heights of ridiculousness when it changed the color of its package and boasted that its former green wrapper "had gone to war." No one quite knew how the green paper was helping beat the Nazis. Despite all the civilian goods taken off the market everyone was living very well. War factories paid big wages, and there was plenty of overtime, often more than the workers wanted. In Britain during the war civilian consumption dropped 22 percent, but in the U.S. it grew.

Everyone in Lockport *knew* they were living at the heart of a vital target that the Nazis would bomb as soon as they finished off London. The canal, we believed, was a *major* objective in the war. True, it wasn't used a whole lot any more for shipping oil or other freight, but still, it *had* to be important. All of us kids used silhouettes printed on cereal boxes to learn to identify German and Japanese warplanes. Adults got in the act, too, and throughout Niagara County, and presumably all across the nation, there were little wooden shanties erected in fields where civilian aircraft spotters probed the sky with field glasses and stood ready to make a phone call that they had sighted enemy aircraft. None ever did, but they made up incidents all the same. Or maybe they were just mistakes. An American Airlines passenger liner could look like a Messerschmitt, couldn't it? Besides, there weren't a whole lot of airliners in the air, with restrictions on gas and most travel limited to essential business.

We were so sure that we were going to be bombed that we had practice blackouts during which we had to put dark curtains over our windows and seal them tightly so that not a smidgen of light escaped. Streetlights and all advertising signs were turned off. Cars still drove with lights, but only their parking lights, which stopped most traffic or brought it to a crawl.

Air raid wardens, equipped with helmets and armbands, patrolled the streets, blowing their whistles sharply if they spotted a bit of light escaping from a window. In school we practiced air raid drills, going to a central corridor of the school and sitting with our backs to the walls and our heads buried between our knees. There was no giggling. This was serious. We could be killed at any moment as soon as the Germans could spare a plane to bomb Lockport's canal locks.

At home we had spots mapped out as air raid shelters, too, and these were stocked with bottled water, blankets, flashlights and spare batteries, canned food and hand-operated can openers.

The war effort seemed to get 100 percent civilian cooperation, but there were occasional rumors of people who were able to get extra ration tickets in some unknown way. Still we were all doing our bit looking for enemy planes, collecting old newspapers, saving grease, and not using our cars when we didn't absolutely have to.

Every year my dad sold a little less bread. "Everybody wants the bread from the big bakeries in Buffalo," he'd say. Their bread was more consistent than Hugo's, softer and better wrapped. And in truth, it wasn't unknown to find a little souvenir left by a mouse in a loaf of Hugo's bread. That wasn't very good for business either. The "Buffalo bread" had the consistency of sponge rubber, and a whole loaf could be squeezed down into a little ball, but people bought it and left the Hugo bread on the shelf.

Nevertheless, the Niagara Baking Co. struggled on, but by the time World War II involved America the business had sagged to an ebb. However, worse was still to come—rationing. Just like everyone in America, bakeries had trouble getting flour, shortening, and sugar, as well as tires and gasoline for the trucks. Hugo could no longer stay in business, so he and his partner turned the truck garage into a machine shop to make some kind of military parts. My dad worked in the shop until the end of the war. He didn't have to race from truck to store and back again, but he missed his old customers and the freedom to make little side trips on personal errands while on the route. The job in the machine shop wasn't one he enjoyed, but, he reasoned, it was wartime and everybody had to do his part.

On May 7, 1945, Germany surrendered, partly as a result, I was convinced, of the war stamps I had bought and the other things I had done to help the war effort. The end of the war in Europe was tagged V-E Day, and celebrations broke out around the world (except in Germany, Italy, and Japan, of course.) I deserved to celebrate, too, to mark our glorious victory. Like about half of my classmates, I skipped school that afternoon and spent the time riding my bike around town. Nobody had gotten a new bike in four years, but our old ones were still running fine.

The next day the roof fell in. The school principal announced over the PA system that he was circulating a list of everybody who had failed to report for school the previous afternoon, and everybody whose name was on the list would have to make up the time at the rate of two hours for every one that had been missed unless they could get an excuse from their parents. I didn't even try and stayed an hour after school every day for the next week and a half.

When the war with Japan ended, fortunately, it was summer vacation.

Chapter 8

FEUDS AND FUMES

I promised you that I'd tell you about the neighbors who lived next to us on the south side, the Kastners. It will be a sad chapter but one that should be told just so you understand.

My parents moved into the Waterman Street house about 1928, I think and Sam and Alma Kastner built the house next door about the same time. They were both young couples trying to get ahead in the world, my dad by selling bread and Sam painting cars at a collision shop. My mother and Alma must have been friendly in those days. There are pictures of them together in my family photo album.

Soon Sam wanted to open his own auto paint shop and what better place than in his own back yard? He could build a big garage there that would take in almost the whole lot, leaving only a little parking area between the house and the garage. Then he'd be his own boss, Alma could help with the work, and they'd achieve the great American dream of having their own business.

Sam had to get a building permit for the big garage, and some kind of permission to operate a shop far outside Lockport's business area. The latter probably wasn't too hard. There were other businesses in houses—a fish market on one of the nicest streets, doctors with offices in their homes, and even a neighbor of ours who had enlarged his house on Willow Street into a dry cleaning shop. And, of course, little grocery stores flourished in residential neighborhoods.

Our neighbors didn't like the idea of the paint shop opening and circulated a petition against it. Sam and Alma pleaded with my parents not to sign it. They were friends, and both young couples were trying to get ahead, so my parents agreed not to sign. Since they would be the closest neighbors to the paint shop and didn't object to it, the project was allowed to proceed.

The one-story wooden garage was built, filling Kastner's entire back yard, stretching maybe 60 feet long. There was space to work on a lot of cars at once and park a few others in a little crushed-stone parking area outside. Kastner had a good reputation for his work, although nobody wanted to cross him and complain about any of it. He was a great bull of a man, short, fat, with arms and legs like tree limbs and a bald head that sat directly on his shoulders without benefit of a neck. He was the neighbor who protested about our flashing Christmas lights. Eventually my father came to refer to him as Ferdinand, the Bull, from some cartoon character of the time.

I don't know when the paint shop became obnoxious, but I suppose it was when the first car was painted. Before being painted the cars were sanded with wet sandpaper. You know what an unpleasant sound that is, and it was always done in the outdoor lot, just a little way from our dining room and bedroom windows and the back door that led into our kitchen. All day long and often until quite late at night that disturbing sanding noise went on. Sam and Alma worked long hours.

At some time, I don't know when or why, the two families had a falling out, and after it happened there was no turning back, no forgiveness on either side. My dad learned that since he hadn't signed the petition to keep the paint shop out before it opened there was nothing he could do now.

Ferdinand became more and more unpleasant as a neighbor and forbid Alma to talk to my mother any more. My dad had planted a row of bushes on the property lines between our house and Edna Stockwell's on one side, Kastner's on the other. My dad trimmed and shaped them into graceful hedges with hand shears. No stray branches were permitted anywhere. On his side, though, Ferdinand cut the bushes into a severe vertical line, destroying their graceful taper.

Whenever Ferdinand found a paper on his grass he assumed that it came from our yard so he poked it through the hedge. I retaliated by sticking some long shears through his fence. Some of his prized flowers just happened to get in the way of the blades. You could have heard his cursing a block away, but he didn't come over to accuse us.

We enjoyed sitting on our front porch but didn't want to be next to Ferdinand and Alma if they ever came out on theirs, so we put up a screen made of dark green wooden slats. It rolled down from the roof of the porch to the floor, and, being on the south side of the house, not only blocked our view of the Kastners and them of us but also shaded us from the sun. Everyone knew that it was a kind of spite fence, though.

These were just little skirmishes in the war of the neighbors. The chemical warfare was the most obnoxious. Ferdinand always arranged to be spray painting a car just when we were eating dinner. He was even more diligent if we happened to be having a picnic in our backyard. Wheels were always painted outside so that his stone driveway could absorb the overspray. The air turned colored, based on whatever paint he was using.

Worse was the smell. If you have ever used a can of spray paint you know the odor and how the fumes spread. It is even worse when the paint is sprayed by compressed air. We usually had to close all of our windows, and with no air conditioning in the summer it wasn't pleasant. On very hot nights we packed a picnic and took it to Outwater Park, on the edge of a bluff where there was always a cool breeze, and far from the paint fumes.

None of the other neighbors were friendly with Ferdinand or Alma either, but the painters kept busy night and day sanding and spraying. There never seemed to be any shortage of cars to be painted. Occasionally we'd hear some loud words—very loud, especially from Ferdinand—when some customer may have remarked about a bill being too high or a surface needing a touch more paint.

Guess whose house was the target of Halloween pranks. It was a wonder that Ferdinand didn't chase us with a baseball bat. I seem to remember that he did once, but that may be creative memory, invented to make the whole affair seem more vicious than it was.

Ferdinand's daughter, Alice, was only a few years younger than me but association with me was frowned on, of course, more so as time went on and the family feud heated up. When we were young we used to play together. She had no back yard, and Ferdinand wouldn't allow anybody to step on his postage stamp front lawn, not even Alice. He'd sit on the porch and yell at them. If some dog got loose he'd have a tantrum, but mostly the dogs just left their calling cards and sauntered on.

Given the holiness of Ferdinand's grass, Alice came over to my house, but we stayed in front so Ferdinand wouldn't see her from the paint shop and start yelling. Even then she was a tease in her skimpy little sundress. I was young but not too young to have some tiny bit of tingle in my pants, although I had no idea what it meant.

Eventually Alice was kept in the house or sent to a reform school or some place by her parents. I never saw her anymore.

When I was a late teen-ager word trickled in that Ferdinand was moving his painting business to Buffalo and the house had been sold. The buyers were a young couple expecting their first baby. His family owned an old established stationery business in Lockport. They were wonderful neighbors. The paint shop stayed but was idle. Maybe Freddie Laux, the new neighbor, stored some of the store's inventory there, but it was quiet and gave off no smell.

Where Ferdinand had been a recluse, except for chasing people off his grass, Freddie loved to meet all the neighbors and joke with them. His great story was about when his wife went into labor pains early and he had to rush her to the hospital for the delivery. She left him to can the bushel of tomatoes she'd just bought.

Freddy was working away diligently, if inexpertly, in the hot kitchen when his dentist's assistant called to remind him of an appointment that day. Freddy proclaimed very flustered, "Madam, I can't go to the dentist. I'm canning my tomatoes." Not a word about the new baby.

Chapter 9

SCHOOL

I liked school, was very fond of reading, and loved my pencil box with its two bright yellow pencils, little red sharpener, curving protractor that I didn't know how to use, a few crayons, and a six-inch blue wooden ruler. The box, made of bright blue cardboard, was held together very neatly with a gold-colored snap. It was a prize possession.

Doris and Audrey went to a Lutheran School, Jimmy and Howard went to St. Mary's Catholic School, and Jack went to St. John's Catholic School after kindergarten. Neither St. Mary's nor St. John's had kindergartens, and New York's school laws didn't require kids to attend them. The Garlocks went right into first grade, but Jack went to kindergarten with me. We walked together every morning to the John E. Pound Elementary School on High Street.

The school was only a few years old when we started, but it is still standing more than 60 years later and looks the same except for its new windows. The red brick two-story building was stately, conservative, and solid, just like Lockport. The playground was just a big dirt lot with hardly any play equipment. The most important piece of apparatus was the bicycle rack.

Jack and I were too little to ride our tricycles to school, but we weren't too little to walk—with one of our mothers going along for the first few weeks to make sure we didn't get lost. Eventually we went by ourselves for the half-day sessions.

Our teacher was Miss Gorman. I was in love with her. I suppose some of the other boys were, too, but I was the one who was going to marry her if she'd wait for me to grow up.

Kindergarten, of course, had to do with sitting on little chairs which we arranged in a circle with much difficulty and reorganized for story time. Then there were scissors and crayons; the big, big sandbox full of toys; papers to draw on and color. And books. It was a wonderful world.

There were lots of cutting, pasting and coloring projects, Halloween pumpkins to draw and color, Christmas chains to cut out and paste together, and then Valentines to make.

Miss Gorman made it very clear that we were to have a valentine for everybody in the class, even the awful girls that Jack and I would only play with if Miss Gorman made us. We made valentines for our mothers and fathers in the class, but making 30 or so for the rest of the kids would have taxed us, and Miss Gorman's patience, beyond the breaking point, so our mothers took us to the five and ten cent store to buy valentines, a dozen to a package complete with envelopes. I carefully signed my name to each of the 30 valentines. On the big day we all walked around the room putting a valentine on everyone's chair.

School ended just before noon, so we struggled into our leggings, boots, coats, hats, scarfs, and mittens. There were great folding doors at the side of the room that opened to reveal little cubicles with hooks for all of our winter clothes. Poor Miss Gorman; she had to sort out 30 pairs of boots, 60 mittens, assorted hats, coats, scarfs, and leggings every day.

We each gathered up our 30 valentines, plus one nice one from Miss Gorman, and put them in our mittened hands. Most of the cards were glossy and hard to hang onto, so we had a bit of difficulty getting them all together.

Finally, everyone was ready, and we trooped in two lines, boys in one, girls in the other, to the school's side door. I think the front doors were reserved for company, just as at home. Out we went into the winter weather. It had been snowing. As a matter of fact it had also been raining and freezing, making the streets and sidewalks like skating rinks.

Jack and I started down John Street for home. Then he fell down, and his valentines scattered on the snow. We scrambled to pick them up with our mittens. When he was back on his feet we took two steps, and I fell down. My valentines went flying, and my mittens didn't bend except under great pressure. My mother had made them of the thickest wool she could find. She wasn't going to have her precious only son get cold hands or have icy water from a melting snowball penetrate his mittens. Consequently recovery of the spilled valentines was a slow and difficult process.

Finally I gathered up my stray valentines with Jack's help, although we had to be careful not to get his and mine mixed. When I was finally erect we proceeded toward home again. I don't remember which of us fell down next. Maybe we both did. Anyway, we were up and down often. Valentines were in the snow more than they were in our mittens.

In the warmth of the school Miss Gorman peered out the window at us, hiding behind the drape so we wouldn't see her. She doubled up with laughter. We didn't know that at the time, of course, but she related the whole incident to my mother later at a PTA meeting. She watched and watched as the whole pitiful incident worked its way to a conclusion, which came when my mother arrived in the car. She couldn't imagine why Jack and I hadn't gotten home from school yet and so set out in search of us.

She found us on our hands and knees only a couple hundred feet from the school door, bundled us into the car, gathered up all the stray valentines, and drove us home. I don't know about Jack, but my mittens were soaked, and my snow pants were even wet inside because of all the crawling around we had done on the semi-frozen tundra. The cat was chased off the dining room register, and my mittens were laid there to dry; the snow pants were hung in the cellar; and my mother and I sat down to a nice bowl of homemade vegetable soup while I related the whole horrible experience. As for Miss Gorman, she never did get any lunch that day, but that was her own fault. She spent her whole lunch period watching Jack and me.

After our kindergarten year all the Catholic kids went to parochial school, and the rest of us advanced to first grade. There had been morning and afternoon kindergartens, but when they were combined for first grade, minus the kids who had gone to Catholic school, there were too many of us for one room.

The school was overcrowded, and there wasn't an extra classroom for another first grade. The principal, Miss McCarthy, who ruled like a czarina from a far office where we never ventured to go, made a decision. The small group, mine, was to use what had formerly been the school clinic as a classroom.

It was a narrow room with only one window. The little hospital cot had been removed and replaced by desks. There were real school desks, not the kindergarten chairs we were used to. The desks had a writing surface that opened to reveal a place where stuff could be stored. We soon learned that if we opened the top and seemed to be searching for something underneath we could sneak a bite of candy.

The chair was fastened to a bent steel rod, so that it could only be swiveled a little bit left and right, not moved forward or backward. And we couldn't tilt back in our chairs. Eventually we got a classroom somewhere that had free-standing chairs, and we all learned how to lean back and tip over, one at a time so that there was a frequent, but not constant, disruption of the classroom. But this was years later, certainly not in first grade. Even if we could have caused a disruption, we were too scared to do it.

There was no blackboard in our clinic-classroom. A portable board was moved in, a tipsy affair that had a chalkboard on one side and a corkboard on the other. It swiveled top over bottom. The writing area was small, so the teacher had to write and erase, write and erase.

I'm glad we didn't have such a board when we got to high school and took chemistry The teacher there loved to write complicated chemical equations that wound around three sides of the room. He understood them, he said, which is more than any of the rest of us did.

But back to first grade. Since the portable blackboard could be tilted, the teacher tipped it for ease of writing. Then somebody complained that they couldn't see because of the reflected light. The board was adjusted. Now it was angled wrong for somebody else.

The room was a bit dark since it had only one narrow window and one light fixture hanging from the ceiling. None of the classrooms in John E. Pound School were brilliantly lighted, but the others at least had five windows that went almost from the floor to the ceiling. Our room was also stuffy. It didn't have the built-in ventilators that regular classrooms had. If the window was opened our papers blew away, and our mothers complained that we were going to catch cold. If the window was closed the room got too warm and we fell asleep.

Somehow we got through the first half of the year and then by some miracle there was a vacant classroom with five windows, light fixtures, regular blackboards, and regulation closets for our coats.

John E. Pound School was segregated with lower grades on the first floor, higher grades, up to sixth, on the second level. Once a week each grade went to the gym. The school board had tried to save money when the school was built by building a gym floor with a stage at one side. This was supposed to work as a place for games or performances and didn't serve either function well. During basketball games the ball went onto the stage, causing a time out. At plays the flat floor made it hard for people in the back to see. Given the sophistication of our productions, the people in the back seats were the lucky ones. They could doze.

The school had no gym coach, so the athletic program was up to each teacher to provide for the class. There was a school band, and so once in a while we were all marched into the gym, now equipped with folding chairs, to hear them wail away on their horns. My father had once played the saxophone and had been a member of an all saxophone band of some 30 or 40 players. Fortunately, it was out of business before I was born, so I never had to listen to it play. I do have a group photo. Wouldn't that have been dreadful to hear 30 or 40 amateur saxophonists at once? Maybe not quite as awful as two bagpipes, but bad enough.

Since my father had been a musician, he wanted me to play an instrument, too, and took me to Mr. Barone, who mostly gave private lessons but also led the school band. Mr. Barone looked at my teeth and said they weren't right for some kinds of horns, and so that was the end of my musical career. I think my parents might have been relieved by this diagnosis because music lessons would have cost money they didn't have. For some reason other types of instruments were never considered.

The only musical device in our house was a radio and a hand-cranked record player called a Victrola that was stored in the cellar along with a stack of 78 rpm records, all dance music of the 1920s. Sometimes I'd go down cellar, crank the machine, put on a record, and lead the band. I don't know why the Victrola was relegated to the cellar and why my parents stopped buying music about the time I came along. I guess they thought their dancing days were over.

Grade school went marching on year by year. It seems strange to think about it now, but where were the hated members of the Pine Street Gang at school? Unless they were all Catholics or Lutherans, they would also have gone to the John E. Pound Elementary School. I guess gangs were for summer vacations, but school was serious business.

We stayed with the same teacher all day except when the visiting music and handwriting teachers made their rounds. Music was singing without accompaniment since most rooms had no piano. The teacher had a little shiny round disk with holes in the edge into which she would blow to give us the pitch. She might as well have been pitching a softball for all I could tell the difference, but that note was supposed to start us off right. "Row, row, row your boat gently down the stream..."

She got about that far and held up her hand for silence. "Frank Bredell, let me hear you sing the line by yourself," she said.

"Row, row, row your boat..."

"That's enough," she said. "You just listen. Every singing group needs an audience, so you be part of the audience." Thus ended my singing career.

She swelled the audience with a few more non-voices, then proceeded with her lesson.

The handwriting teacher, Miss Quinn, was more of a pain. She expected me to be able to write perfectly between two lines on the paper with excellent Palmer method penmanship. If I could have found out who that Palmer was I'd have strangled him.

Miss Quinn was a prim and proper lady in a black dress that came down nearly to her high-top shoes and always wore a flat, lacy white collar. Most noticable were her little black-rimmed glasses that stayed on by pinching the bridge of her nose. They had no pieces that went over her ears but dangled from a long black cord when she wasn't wearing them.

Our writing paper had lines one half inch apart, a dark line, a light line, like that all down the page. We were to write between the dark lines, which were an inch apart. Each of our pens had a steel point that was jammed into a wooden holder by the blunt end. The point was then dipped into a little ink well that was inserted into a hole in each desk. Miss Quinn showed us the proper writing technique. "Dip your pen in the ink, tap the point gently on the edge of the ink well to shake off extra ink, place the point of the pen lightly on the paper with the handle pointing at your tie," she'd recite. None of us wore a tie, but maybe Miss Quinn thought we should or didn't want to use a coarse word like chest, or heaven forbid, breast.

"Now put the pen point on the second dark line and push it up to the top, pull down, push up, pull down, push, pull. Slant a little bit to right and keep the pen pointed at your tie. Class, now you try it."

I dipped my pen point in the ink, tapped like she had showed us and put the tip on my paper. A big ink blot spread out as I looked at it horrified. Fortunately I had a piece of blotting paper for just such an occasion, but it only took up the liquid ink, not what had already been absorbed by the paper.

I tried again. It was a little better this time. No blot. I began to make push-pulls, but my pushes went above the top line and my pulls below the bottom. I kept trying, but they got no better.

Miss Quinn strolled up and down the aisles correcting the aim of a pen here, praising the strokes there, suggesting a little more pressure, maybe a little less. "Dip your pen again when the writing gets too light," she counseled. Everything was going well apparently.

Then she walked slowly past my desk and stopped. Up came the glasses to her nose and she bent over my paper. She was so alarmed at what she saw that the glasses sprung off her nose and dangled by the string. Trying to recover and calm herself, she placed her hand on mine and pushed my hand into two or three perfect push-pulls.

"There," she said. "That's the way."

She took her hand away as I continued to saw up and down. My pen still went outside the lines. Whenever I dipped it in the ink there was a chain of tiny, messy blots leading from ink well to wherever I had left off pushing and pulling. She made another attempt at guidance, and all was well, but left to my own devices my push-pulls were still hopeless.

Miss Quinn gave up and went to the front of the room. "Now we'll do ovals," she said and demonstrated perfectly on the blackboard, making what looked like a long tightly coiled spring, exactly within the lines she had drawn.

This was a little more fun, but the "nice rounded ovals" she told us to make came out a little squashed when I tried them. They looked more like broken eggs.

Miss Quinn drifted around the room nodding in appreciation of the fine penmanship she was instilling in us. Then she came to me.

"I think that will be all for today," she said, trying to regain her composure. "Take two sheets of the paper home and practice. Your teacher will collect them tomorrow so I can see them." She turned and left, but unfortunately she came back the next week, and the next and the next after that, all year. Try as I might, my push-pulls and ovals never met her approval.

Never had anyone devised such an instrument of torture as those pens we had to use. Even the girls who had nice neat push pulls and ovals had trouble with them. They were scratchy and very hard to control so that they didn't make blots. If there was too much ink they made a great smeary mess. Too little, and there were no letters at all. And the noise of 30 students scratching away with them! Maybe that was why our regular teacher disappeared for the hour or so that Miss Quinn was with us. The only good thing was that the pens gave girls a chance to cut up pieces of cloth to make pen wipers. Oh yes, the pen point had to be cleaned before it was put away.

Eventually the class graduated to making nice rounded written letters, but I think Miss. Quinn gave up on me and just kept walking when she came down the aisle next to my desk. To this day her effort shows. My handwriting is illegible, even to me.

Every fall, then as now, there was the strange American phenomenon called the World Series. If there was pro football, pro hockey, or pro anything else I didn't know it, but baseball was supposed to be important. It was so important that during the Series every teacher drew a scoreboard on her blackboard near the classroom door.

During the game the janitor listened to the radio in his little supply room, and at the end of every half inning made the rounds of every classroom and wrote the score for that half inning on the board. The teacher's lesson was totally disrupted by cheers and boos every time a new number was posted.

Other items of vital importance were communicated to each classroom by a sixth grade honor student who carried a memo from the office around to each room every afternoon. This also disrupted the lesson as the teacher read the memo to see if it was something that she ought to read to us or was some inside stuff that we weren't supposed to know about. The sixth grader had read the memo on the way to the first classroom, of course, so whatever private information it contained was relayed to everyone after school.

At the end of sixth grade we were ready to move on to junior high school. There was no ceremony, no mock graduation, nothing. Maybe the teachers went out of town somewhere, or more likely to someone's house, pulled the shades and lifted a few in celebration of another bunch of idiots out of the way. No drinking was done by teachers in public. Not ever.

Chapter 10

JUNIOR HIGH AND HIGH SCHOOL

Lockport had some half
dozen public elementary schools, but only two junior high
schools, both near the edge of the city, one in the far
north, the other in the south. I went to the southern
school, Emmett Belknap Junior High School. It was a dis-
tinguished looking U-shaped red brick building topped by
a large, white cupola. It could almost have been a county
courthouse or some other important edifice. It still looks
the same, standing importantly at the end of its long oval
driveway.

Belknap was farther away than my grade school, so now
I rode my bike to school whenever the weather was decent
and often when it wasn't. Sometimes I'd almost have to
push the bike to get through the snow. It would have been
easier to walk on those days, but by now I had a paper route

and needed the bike or some other vehicle to carry the papers, which were very heavy. But more about that later.

By now I also had a new bike, a shiny black Schwinn with gleaming white trim, big balloon tires, a kick stand, rear reflector, front headlight (although I wasn't supposed to be out on it after dark), the whole works. It was a wonderful machine. I polished it nearly every day and kept it locked to the bicycle rack at school.

Ready to roll on a new Schwinn.

One day a roofing company came to the school to tar the roof. Their tar kettle gave off ugly, choking fumes that made it hard to breathe nearby, but worse than anything, the tar smoke turned my bicycle's snow white trim muddy yellow. I was horrified and then so angry I could have kicked the tar pot over. No amount of scrubbing, bleaching or pretending could restore the white. It was some sort of a lesson that sometimes bad things happen that can't be avoided, but I was still mad.

Junior high school was different in many ways from John E. Pound Elementary. There were more kids for one thing and lots of them from other grade schools. Some even had Italian names, something that we'd never had at John E. Pound. A few came from wealthier families and talked about things I didn't have—a telephone, a second car, extended summer trips.

Also, we now moved from room to room instead of having the same teacher all day. All those kids shifting around every hour had the potential for creating chaos, but not as long as Ralph R. Shattuck was principal of Emmett Belknap. He would have been happy running a Nazi prison, but since he apparently couldn't get a job doing that he tried to create a prison atmosphere in the school.

He must have liked to hear loud bells. There was an early bell in the morning that told the janitors to unlock the doors for first students. Then there was a five minute warning bell. Then a bell for the start of school and another one minute later that meant anyone not in his seat would be marked tardy and have to be duly punished.

Two minutes before the end of each class there was another bell. That excused the hall monitors from their classes so they could take up their posts before the stampede of students changing classes. That two-minute warning, I supposed, was also to alert teachers to sum up what they were saying. In effect it told everyone to pack up books and papers, quit paying attention, and get ready to bolt out of the classroom.

Five minutes later there was another bell that signaled the start of the next class and told the hall monitors to turn off most of the corridor lights and go off duty. The day went on and on like that with bells ringing every few minutes. And they weren't little chimes either but clanging fire bells.

Since gym classes were sometimes held outside on the athletic fields, bells were installed outside the school and could be heard all over the area. They probably drove the neighbors crazy. Summers must have been a blessed relief.

The hall monitors were mostly ninth graders, Belknap's highest grade, and honor students as well. They were supposed to be smart enough so they could afford to get out of every class two minutes early. Teachers had to make sure not to give out homework assignments during those last minutes.

The monitors wore red and white armbands, the school colors, and were charged with making everybody walk to the right and use 90-degree angles when turning a corner into a classroom or down another corridor. There was a sergeant who patrolled and made sure the other monitors were performing up to snuff. Anybody who was not enforcing the proper discipline and respect for the armbands was relieved of duty very quickly without a trial. I got to be a monitor for a while, but it really wasn't what I wanted to be in life. After that the thought of joining the military or the police turned me off.

If Mr. Shattuck could have gotten away with making us

goose step, he would probably have done it, but World War II was raging at this time, and things German were out of favor.

Just as a side note, eight years after I left Emmett Belknap School, I read about Mr. Shattuck in a Westchester County, New York, newspaper. He had been superintendent of schools in one of the county's wealthy cities and was being fired.

But back to my school days. After the bell rang that was supposed to signal the start of the day's first class there would be some trumpet blasts over the school public address system. The blasts were created by one of the school's horn players who was giving what he thought was a little fanfare to start the day and get everyone's attention. Sometimes the trumpet player got the notes almost right.

Then everyone was to stand and turn toward Mecca. Oh, excuse me. We were just to face the front of the room and say the Pledge of Allegiance together. That done, we could sit down and the lesson could begin, but not quite yet. A student had a few announcements to read over the PA in a boring, stumbling voice. "The pep rally will be held Thursday, excuse me, Friday at 3:30 o'clock after school on the practice field. Smearleaders, excuse me, cheerleaders will be excused from classes at 3:18. Blah, blah, blah."

Now for the lesson? Not yet. Our master's voice came on the PA with more good news. "The quarterly report cards will be sent home this Friday. You must have your card signed by your parent and returned to school on Monday without any excuse." No parent had better be out of town, in the hospital, or have any other reason for not signing that report card.

Then came a harangue about how we had failed to march in two straight lines yesterday and there was (oh horrors) a candy wrapper found in the hallway outside the cafeteria. Anyone caught throwing any kind of wrapper on the floor would get one week of detention. That meant they had to stay one hour after school every day for a week. Some poor teacher had to babysit the roomful of kids who were in detention for committing one grievous crime or another.

Detention was supposed to be a good time to do homework, and sometimes some of us detainees actually opened books and picked up pens. By the way, we had now abandoned the dip-and-tap-into-the-inkwell type of pens in favor of cheap ballpoints. We had to buy our own ballpoints, but the school provided paper and pencils. Why the discrimination? I didn't know.

Emmett Belknap had an interesting mix of teachers. Nell Van Wyck taught math, just as she had when my father was one of her pupils. She was well past her prime, he said, when he had her as a teacher, so that tells you something about her age when I was in her class. Nevertheless, she tried to dress like a teen-ager—too-short plaid skirt, too-tight sweater, and bobby socks.

She was as sharp as a tack about math but a bit muddled about everything else and cross-eyed as well. She had a habit of rapping her finger loudly on the desk and shouting out the name of a student who was then to stand and recite. The trouble was that Nell's fingers were all misshapen from years and years of rapping, and when she pointed you weren't sure if it was at you or somebody in the next aisle. She never looked at where she was pointing, so it got really confusing.

She spieled off an arithmetic problem as fast as she could talk: "Six times three divided by nine is what? Robert Bluett stand and recite." Rap would go the finger. It pointed at Robert Blount, so he got out of his seat. But she had said Bluett so Warren Bluett also stood. Nell looked from one to the other trying to remember which name she had called, then totally confused, sort of pointed at one of them and said, "You, you sit down." That left the other one to answer the question, except that everyone had now forgotten what it was.

When I told my dad about this stuff, he laughed. "That's just the way Nell was when I was in school," he said.

There were a couple of other teachers that I especially remember for their peculiarities, a mother and daughter team, Maud and Frances Sipson. They lived together and drove to school in a spiffy Cord convertible automobile, an ancient machine that hadn't been manufactured in years. I had never seen another and still haven't outside a museum. I suppose it could have been a collector's item, or just another way for them to express their individuality. The Cord was always parked in front of the school, headed east so they could make a quick getaway to go home.

The huge car had a control panel that looked like it could have been in a modern jetliner. There were dozens of knobs, handles, and little dials. If anyone had paid attention to all the little dials, there would have been no time to watch the road. Maybe that's why the Sipsons traveled together, one to watch the dials, the other to drive.

The Cord was notable for being hard to start. I suppose all of those knobs and handles had to be tweaked just right to get the fool thing to fire up all of its eight or maybe 12 cylinders. Our lunch hours were adequate but not long enough if you had to undertake a major endeavor to get your car started and drive home and back. Maud, the mother part of the Dynamic Duo, always hid behind the door of her classroom, already bundled in her hat, coat, and gloves about ten minutes before it was time to leave for lunch. The door had glass panels, so she had to stand well back so the principal wouldn't see her hiding there if he passed. She made sure the long plume on her hat didn't give her away, and we all had to keep quiet so no one in the hall would hear her talking right up next to the door.

We sat quietly watching the clock. The minute hand moved by jumps. Suddenly it jumped to 11:45, time to leave for lunch, and the bell clanged. No one was allowed to move until Mrs. Sipson had gained at least a 10-foot head start. She drew open the door with the casual movement of an actress reluctantly leaving the stage and sashayed out. Once at the school door, which fortunately for her, was only a few steps away, she bolted for the car and began going through the checklist of maneuvers to get it started. Her daughter must have also been hiding in her classroom. She appeared seconds later, and as soon as the monster automobile exploded into life they were gone in a noisy cloud of dust.

My mother and father were so intrigued by my tales of the Dynamic Duo that they began to wonder where they lived and investigated. I suppose they did that by looking in the phone book or the city directory that the bakery had. At any rate, one day while we were driving around Lockport we hunted up their house. It was in Carlyle Gardens, a very exclusive neighborhood on the east edge of Lockport across from the country club. We wondered how two teachers could afford such a grand house.

I only remember one thing that Maud Sipson taught, and that probably should have been forgotten. She said it was good to eat mold from bread and cheese because mold is what penicillin comes from. She vowed that she'd never get sick because she was getting all that natural antibiotic.

Her daughter, Frances, taught algebra. She spent no time whatever trying to make us understand the principles behind the calculations but insisted that we learn her "handy-Andy method for nitwits." To her credit, I can still make some quick math calculations, but don't ask me for any theories.

Both of the Dynamic Duo wore so much red rouge on their faces that they looked like they were performing in a circus.

Emmett Belknap School required all boys to take a shop course to give us a little exposure to such trades as machine shop, metalworking, woodworking, and printing. That was probably a good idea, since a large proportion of our students would end up working in factories or trades.

I liked printing best and once even made rounds of Lockport's print shops looking for part-time work, which I never got. The shops didn't know it, but they were lucky. As my printing course went on I found it quite easy to spill whole pages of handset type on the table. This kept me busy for several class periods picking up each piece, deciphering it, and putting it back in the right compartment of the type tray.

In metalworking class the little funnel I made of light sheet metal turned out to be oval instead of round, the spout went at a peculiar angle, and the neat rolled edge at the top was neither neat nor rolled. Mostly it was just bent down and hammered flat.

I moved on to wood shop, where I cut a block of wood and spun it on a lathe until it was round, grooved, and shiny. I gave it a nice coat of stain and varnish, cut another piece of wood into a triangle, and the whole business was then assembled to make a hanging lamp. It was a decent first effort, even though the varnish never dried entirely, leaving the wood a bit sticky. And the whole apparatus fell off the wall whenever touched.

I spent so much time with the printing, funnel, and lamp that I never got to run the machines that were supposed to help me make some metal object that no doubt would have been entirely useless.

Mr. Beck, the shop teacher who had to cope with all of these crafts, was a bit hard of hearing, and I was never sure he had really understood the questions I asked. He may have given the right answer to the wrong question. I liked him though. In his spare time, for extra money, he fixed radios, and I took a couple to his house for repairs. His diagnosis was always the same, "It needs filters." Maybe he was right. The sound was marginally better after he tinkered.

I also took another elective course that wasn't as much of a disaster as shop. That was a course called "homemaking for boys." The school had a model apartment (no bedroom, of course; we couldn't have any hint of scandal) but with a furnished living room and two kitchens, one with a gas stove, the other with an electric model. I vacuumed and dusted, learned about simple food ingredients, and made brownies that were good, if a bit dry. I also cut out and sewed my own apron. My blind grandmother couldn't have done a whole lot better. Anyway, it kept the flour off my blue corduroy pants, and I passed the homemaking course.

The most feared of all teachers was Mr. Blakesley, who taught science but was renowned as enforcer of discipline along with Mr. Shattuck. Mr. Blakesley had some shop students in a previous class make a wooden paddle for him, about 12 inches long, 10 inches wide with about a 10-inch handle. It looked like an overgrown ping pong paddle, only thicker. It was made of two pieces of wood with space between them. When he swung the paddle and hit something, it gave off a smacking sound that could be heard half a block away.

The somethings he hit were the bottoms of the students, mostly boys, but sometimes girls as well. The offender leaned over the laboratory table, and the resulting noise and pain almost sent him leaping over it. Paddling was usually limited to one whack and always administered in full view of the class. Mr. Blakesley's face let us know that he loved the whole procedure. Fortunately I was only a witness, not a participant, in this barbaric activity. Mr. Shattuck was also reputed to have a paddle in his office, which he administered in the same way to serious offenders.

Every Wednesday afternoon those of us who had our parents' signed permission got out of school an hour and a half early so we could go to our own churches for religious instruction. Those who didn't participate could stay in the school study hall or library.

Beany Blount and I rode our bikes to Emanuel Methodist Church. His real name was Bob, but everyone called him Beany for the little cap he wore. Getting to the church shouldn't have taken us any more than 10 minutes, but we had one difficulty and had to make a detour. Blount loved trains. He had model trains in his basement, he read train magazines, and decided that we had to go past the church a few blocks to the old railroad station to see if there was a train. There never was, but there were several sets of tracks and sometimes a boxcar standing idle.

We looked up and down the tracks and put our ears to a rail to see if we could hear a train coming. We'd seen that trick in the movies, but we never heard anything. Then we'd go inside the station and see what activity there was. I think the last passenger ticket had been sold maybe 10 years earlier and all the freight activity had been moved somewhere else, so the place wasn't what you could call lively. Nevertheless, we had to check the bulletin boards to see if they held any important railroad news or a schedule that we hadn't noticed in our inspection the previous week. There was a schedule that had been posted so long ago that it had turned yellow. Everywhere the typewriter had written an o, the paper had disintegrated and left a little hole.

Finally we turned up the hill and rode the two blocks to church. Our class had begun quite some time earlier, and the teacher had inquired about our absence. Everyone testified that we had been in school, so the teacher, a volunteer who was spectacularly unqualified to cope with 12 and 13-year-old boys, was torn between rushing to the minister to report that we must have been kidnapped or just waiting it out. She waited.

Every week was the same routine until finally we were told that we no longer needed to come to religious education classes. We thought maybe we had done so well that we had nothing more to learn.

In the end it turned out OK. Blount went to work for a railroad, a career he pursued until he retired. And I went to theology school evenings for several years, so I made up for what I'd missed at the Methodist Church.

After a three-year sentence at Emmett Belknap I was sent on to Lockport Senior High School. What a difference. First, the building was nearly 100 years old and looked it. In my senior year the school celebrated its centenary. The interior was dark, grim, and poorly lighted, and the walls were dark varnished wainscot.

Floors were made of wood on which any varnish had long since been worn away. The central wide wooden stairway creaked and groaned with every step, and a couple of little side stairways were narrow and mysterious. You had to know what route to take to another part of the building or you'd never get there.

There was a very small gym, too small for regulation basketball, with a banked running track in a balcony above it. The legend among the students was that the gym floor rested on a bed of water. Maybe that was true; there was certainly a bounce to the floor that you could feel.

The ventilating system was antique, like the school. That was unfortunate the day Blount and I tried mixing a few things in the third-floor chemistry laboratory and filled most of the building with choking smoke. No one ever found out who was to blame. Another legend among the students was that the chem lab was on the top floor so that in case of an explosion things would fly out the skylight and save the rest of the building.

The school had a small but very pleasant auditorium with a sloping floor and a little stage. The whole room was painted a creamy white with some bits of gold trim. The lower walls were made up entirely of French doors. Only a couple of them were real doors, and even those didn't go outside, but into corridors. The rest of the doors were fakes that didn't open. All the "doors" had mirrors instead of glass. In a fire people would have panicked trying to yank open things that looked like doors but weren't. It is a wonder the fire marshal, if Lockport had one, didn't order some redecorating to cover the fake doors, but he didn't. There were little exit signs over the real doors, but even those doors wouldn't have been useful if the building had been on fire.

The stage was probably inadequate for theatrical productions, but the theater club made it work somehow. Graduation ceremonies were held next door in the Palace Theater, which had a large auditorium.

The high school had no grounds around it and was located on Lockport's main street. For the good part, it was next to the Palace Theater for those who wanted to skip school; across the street from the YMCA for the jocks; and only half a block away from Castle's ice cream parlor, *the* place to go any afternoon or evening. The parlor had 20 or 30 tables plus a counter for carryout ice cream concoctions and employed lots of students. All the boys had hopes of dating the owner's daughter, blonde Dorothy Castle, who was in my class at school. A few of the boys succeeded but never bragged about getting as far as they hoped.

The bad part of the school's location was its proximity to a factory right across the street. The factory, part of General Motors' Harrison Radiator Division, stamped out parts for auto radiators and heaters. It was very noisy and was separated from the school only by a narrow street. Neither building was air-conditioned, of course, so in the spring and fall, with windows open on both sides of the street, we heard more noise than teachers' voices.

In my mind I can still hear Herr Karp, the German teacher whose windows faced the factory, yelling at an unsure student, *"Was sagts du? Spricht lauter, bitte. Ich kann nicht hören."* ("What are you saying? Speak louder, please. I can't hear you.") After still not being able to hear the mumbled German, he'd give up on getting fresh air and say, *"Macht das Fenster zu."* ("Close the window.")

A couple of us leaped from our seats and yanked the big wooden double-hung window closed. It came down with a crash so hard it was a wonder the glass survived the exercise. There was now a little less noise from the factory, but the ever-present hiss from the steam radiator continued. Teachers had no way to control the temperature in the classrooms, which were either too hot or too cold. The heat came from the city's central steam plant near the school. Ventilation came from opening a window, which was sometimes OK, depending on what side of the building the room was on.

Herr Karp was soon sweating. He yelled out, "*Es ist zu heiss in dieses Klassenzimmer. Öffnet das Fenster noch einmal!*" He was right; it was too hot so we did as he said, sprang to a window again and opened it to let in the noise. The window was so heavy that it took two of us to heave the sash up. Whatever else we learned in German, we understood Fenster, the word for window.

We didn't, unfortunately, learn really useful things, like "Where is the bathroom?" in German, or to interpret a menu—stuff that would really be helpful if traveling in Germany. Instead we learned all about Uncle Karl and his Sunday walks in the Black Forest.

We also learned, not from Herr Karp, but sort of by osmosis, that he was that rare, almost unknown, person in Lockport—a Jew. In addition to being a teacher, he was a part-time rabbi. I didn't know anything about Jews. There were none on Waterman Street, as far as I knew. However, on Willow Street, on the corner of Waterman, lived a Jewish family, the Greenfields. They had a party in their back yard every fall with music, and colored lights strung in the trees. Members of the notorious Waterman Street Gang peered through the bushes, wondering what the celebration was all about. It wasn't until years later that I realized that the Greenfields, and their Jewish friends were celebrating Rosh

Hashanah, the start of the Jewish new year. I wonder now, but didn't then, if Herr Karp was at the parties.

The best thing about the high school was the principal and the teachers. Gone was the Prussian atmosphere of Emmett Belknap. Lloyd McIntyre, the high school principal, was a reasonable sort of man, calm in the face of student antics. Now we'd call him laid back. He didn't enjoy hearing bells as much as Mr. Shattuck had, so few bells rang out every day. He also didn't really care whether we walked on the left or right side of the corridors as we changed classes. There were no hall monitors to make sure that we turned square corners. About all that mattered was that we got to our classes at some reasonable time. There weren't even any more written permission slips to leave the room during classes, as had been the rule at Belknap, so we could go to the bathrooms when we chose to admire their antique plumbing.

He did frown on smoking in the bathrooms and had lectures prepared, which he delivered in his office to the offenders, but I never heard of any swinging, whacking paddles. His dislike of smoking was justifiable, especially since a discarded flaming match might have easily burned down the school. None ever did, though. It went on serving for several more years until it was replaced by a sprawling modern building on the edge of town. The last time I drove past the "new" school, now maybe 30 or 40 years old, there was no ice cream parlor down the street, no nearby YMCA, and no movie house. The school probably does have an adequate gym, though. And no factory across the street. I wonder what the present German teacher does for amusement.

I remember many of the teachers, not for their peculiarities, but because they were good at their jobs. That doesn't mean that they didn't have quirks. If they hadn't had some peculiarities, what would students have snickered about behind their backs?

I'd gotten to like math, despite old Nell and Frances Sipson. I took plane and solid geometry, advanced algebra, trigonometry, and even spherical trigonometry (the latter so I would be able to navigate the boat I was sure to buy sometime). The courses were taught by a gray little man named Guy Travis. He spoke very quietly, not having a room facing the factory, and was very thorough in his teaching methods.

He drilled and drilled, especially using questions that had been asked in recent Regents' examinations. The Regents, for those who never had the good fortune to go to high school in New York State, is a board that sets the standards and determines the curriculum for all public schools in the state. They also issue annual standardized examinations, always just called the Regents' exams. When I had to take them they were dreaded, by teachers and students alike.

We spent at least half of each year answering questions that had appeared on previous exams. If the Regents had asked a question about determining the volume of a cylinder three years ago, was that question ripe for a repeat? What about the question about the effect of Reconstruction on the South after the Civil War? That seemed to be a favorite, so we'd practice writing essays about that. If the Regents ever came up with a question that they had never asked before, we were all in deep trouble, including the teacher who hadn't prepared us properly.

If you graduated from high school with a Regents diploma, it meant that you had passed all of the required Regents' exams and were prepared to enter college. If you weren't headed for college, you could get a lower level diploma that didn't require the exams but also wasn't as highly regarded and didn't open doors to any kind of advanced education, except maybe a trade school. Students who didn't know what they wanted to do after graduation, and that was most of us, were advised to take the Regents' exams, "just in case."

In the math department, Mr. Travis' efforts and mine paid off. I scored 100 percent on both plane and solid geometry Regents exams and very high in other math tests.

Lockport High School when it was new.

Herr Karp was great for two years of German, all that the school offered. I still remember some simple German expressions and even now can recite the opening lines of Schiller's poem, "Die Lorelei"—*Ich weiss nicht was soll es bedeuten das ich so traurig bin*"...I can go on further too through the whole first verse. As a matter of fact 50 years after leaving Lockport High School I recited the verse to an astonished clerk who was operating a postcard shop on an excursion boat going up the Rhine River past the Lorelei mountain in Germany. To make sure that I really knew what I was talking about I bought a postcard that had the full text of the poem in German and a CD with the music that the poem had been set to. The clerk was much impressed by my German, especially when I told him that I had learned it several years before he was born. What else could he say, especially if he was interested in selling me the postcard and CD?

Augusta Metzler, whose personality was abrasive, made me write a decent essay with proper spelling and punctuation. She wouldn't have been able to read my work if I had written it by hand, even using Miss Quinn's push-pulls and ovals. However, somewhere along the line I had taught myself to type and supplemented that with a typing course taught by Eunice Miller, who insisted on absolutely perfect posture at the typewriter and had us practice endlessly the letters F and J to learn where our first fingers were. I think of that now as I slouch over my keyboard.

Trandon Burns taught history and made it interesting even if it did have too many dates to keep straight.

I also took chemistry, assisting Beany Blount in some of

his more exotic experiments, and physics, where the most trouble we could cause was to overflow vessels of water while we were endeavoring to measure volumes of solids. The teacher, Robert Stanton, always wore a lab coat that looked like a raincoat. He had probably had students like Blount and me before.

In gym we'd do the best we could with the scanty facilities the school had, but at least Byron Linville, who taught the boys' classes, never expected great things of us. There were no playing fields around the school and no swimming pool, so we played games and jogged around the running track on the balcony overlooking the little gym. The varsity teams went to Emmet Belknap to practice. I wonder if there were special bells ringing for them.

I once took the notion that I'd like to join the swimming team and went to the try-out. The coach let me practice with the team, but it soon became apparent that I wasn't going to be able to compete successfully, so I dropped out. The coach was relieved.

Part of the health and phys ed program was a course in boys' health. That was taught by a tired little man named Chauncey Cobb, who was the butt of many jokes because he apparently had only one suit to his name, a brown one that he wore every day for the three years I was at the school. Worse, he never taught the sex stuff that as boys we wanted to know about.

The girls' health teacher, Gertrude Wilcox, was a lot more bouncy and varied in her wardrobe. I wonder if she ever taught them the stuff they were dying to find out.

Blount was my best friend in junior high and high school, but I don't think he was terribly popular with his neighbors after he joined the high school band and started to learn how to play the drums. Every day after school the neighbors were treated to a session of unrhythmical pounding of drums. He didn't have a little wooden block to practice on, something that the neighbors couldn't hear. The pounding went on with full sized drums, letting everyone witness the practice.

I liked to visit at his house. His father, Bill, repaired watches at a little workshop in one corner of the dining room. That wasn't his full-time job, just something he did in his spare time to make a little more money. The workbench contained a huge array of tiny watch springs and wheels, most of them in little drawers, but also a big pile in the middle of the desk, where they were being sorted or something.

He liked to tell the story about the time he was fixing an antique pocket watch and had to send to Switzerland for a spring. Packages crossing the Atlantic went by boat and took at least six weeks. I never could figure that out. Ocean liners made the crossing in five days. Where was the package all the rest of the time?

Anyway, six weeks it was and even more figuring in the time it took Blount's dad to get around to writing the letter to the factory, going to the post office for special stamps and his letter crossing the Atlantic.

Finally a package arrived from Switzerland. After opening multiple layers of paper and packing material a tiny spring came into view. After a few more days of delay while Bill planned his attack on the antique watch, the evening for action finally arrived. He sat at his workbench, adjusted the light, and put on his jeweler's magnifying glass, which he wore fastened to a leather band around his head.

He finally pried open the back of the watch and peered in. He lifted out the broken spring with tiny tweezers and positioned the new one carefully. Now all that remained was hooking the ends of the spring through some little holes to keep it stretched in position. One end was easy, since there was no tension on the spring. Now came the hard part, stretching the tiny spring with the tweezers and twisting it ever so slightly to get the wire through the hole.

The delicate operation was all but done when Bill felt a sneeze coming on. He couldn't stop it and let out a mighty blast. His hand shook, the tweezers lost their grip on the spring, and it flew out of the watch. It flew not only out of the watch but landed somewhere near the great pile of watch parts on the workbench. Bill let out more than a few nasty words and called his wife, Agnes, and Bob to help him search for the missing spring. There were lots of little springs in the pile on the desk, and they picked them up one at a time and showed them to Bill. None was the right one for the antique watch.

The search continued and widened to the little drawers of the desk, since in all the confusion of the search no one could remember which, if any, of the little drawers had been open during the unfortunate sneeze. The floor was also searched, and all use of the vacuum cleaner or carpet sweeper was banned until further notice.

The hunt continued for several hours, Bill getting angrier all the time and the air becoming somewhat heavy with naughty words. Finally the operation was called off for the night. The next night it resumed but with no luck. The same thing for a few more nights, until Bill realized that the only thing to do would be to order another spring from Switzerland and wait another six weeks or more for it to arrive. I don't know how he explained all of this to the owner of the watch or who paid for two springs when only one was needed.

Agnes and Bill Blount always told lots of jokes. They also liked to have a drink or two in the evening and always offered Bob and me something. We talked about what kind of alcoholic beverage we wanted but always settled for ginger ale until we graduated from high school. Graduation night set us free of the world of the drys and we joined the wets. We were sorry about it almost as soon as we did it, but it was too late then.

There were a few open house parties on graduation night, and we went from one to the other. We were grown up and had reached the magical age of 18, the age in New York State at that time at which we could legally drink.

Graduation night was warm. It was July 1. Yes, I said July. Education was serious business in Lockport, and we were kept toiling away at it almost until the 4th of July. At one of the graduation parties Blount and I were offered glasses of beer drawn from a keg. I'd never tasted beer before, my parents never having it in the house. When I'd been with Uncle Tonius, Greasy Walker, and Uncle Art during their refreshment stops, I'd been restricted to root beer.

I took a taste of the beer. Aagh. It didn't taste good, but I was now 18 years old and had been for more than a month. It was time to toss down a few, or at least a little bit of one, so I took another sip. It was no better, but I plugged away. When my glass was nearly empty, and I could safely get rid of it the mother of the kid who was giving the party took the glass and refilled it. Whatever could have possessed her?

Anyway I drank the second glass, and Blount did the same. We might even have had part of a third glass before we staggered outside, around the side of the house and threw up in some convenient bushes. We were not yet what you might call sophisticated drinkers, but we practiced that summer and gradually improved our abilities.

Thus my years at Lockport Senior High School ended. I never went back to visit the school after I graduated, and eventually the building was torn down. I don't know what happened to the teachers; I never saw any of them again.

As a matter of fact, I kept in touch with only a handful of the kids who had been in my class. Bob Blount and I stayed friends, although I went off to college and he went first to business school, then to his career on the railroad.

Since I never went to a high school reunion, I didn't learn much about what happened to any of the kids I'd been with for those three years. Some 40 or so years later I was visiting in Lockport and read in the *Union-Sun & Journal* that two of my former classmates had gone to jail for stealing money from the county. One had worked in the jail but was then going to become a full-time guest.

Another of my classmates was police chief in Lockport for a number of years, another was assistant fire chief, and another opened and operated a machine shop, quite profitably, I believe.

In recent years one of my high school girl friends wrote me from Georgia. I don't know what gave her the idea of looking up old classmates. As I remember, she lived in a nice house tucked into a street so narrow that it should have been called an alley. Maybe it was. She and I dated several times, but then she met this high school senior, or maybe he had already graduated and was going to college. I couldn't compete with him.

I suppose I led a very sheltered life, but I never knew of any sexual fooling around in high school, although there were rumors of a girl who had dropped out to have a baby. I was dating Mary Kolb, the boss' daughter, so to speak. He was the one who said whether or not I could have my paper route. I certainly didn't want to be caught messing around with her, and I don't think she would have known what to do, and I certainly didn't.

There was one girl that Blount and I had fantasies about. She had breasts that would match any in Hollywood at the time but unfortunately not the face to go with them. Blount and I talked at length about what it would be like to be in bed with her. Would we bounce on those tits or fall off? We had no idea of how to make an approach to find out, but beyond talk, we weren't really interested. The girl had the worst case of body odor either of us had ever encountered.

Chapter 11

A FEW LESSONS OUT OF SCHOOL

School was OK, but there were a few things of a practical nature that were hard for me to master. One was learning to swim. I didn't care if I learned or not. The only water near us was the canal, and only a handful of the bravest boys ever swam in its polluted water. The beach at Olcott on Lake Ontario was freezing cold and stony besides, and the beaches on the Canadian side of Lake Erie were so shallow that you'd get exhausted by the time you had walked out into water deep enough to swim in.

Nevertheless, my father who couldn't swim and regretted it, determined that I should know how. Thus I was enrolled in a short class at the YMCA. Every Saturday morning I rode my bike downtown to the Y, about a 10-minute venture, and reported to the pool. We stuffed our clothes into little wire baskets which were left unlocked on steel shelves, took soapy showers, and presented ourselves for a close inspection of our bodies by the instructor. He checked very carefully for unwashed dirt and anything that looked like a rash or open sore that might spread disease. We were sent back to the shower for a re-wash if needed. Then I lined up with the other little boys along the edge of the pool.

We weren't allowed to wear swim suits. I suppose they might not have been too clean and would have contaminated the pool, so we stood there naked, shivering in the cold air and peering down into the sparkling water. I have to give the YMCA credit, they kept their pool very, very clean. But the best you could say for the water temperature was that it was "bracing."

The instructor ordered us into the water along the shallow side of the pool just to get wet and used to the water. That was enough for me. I was ready to get out and go home. However, nothing would do but we had to practice some exercises that would turn us into swimmers. "Take hold of the edge of the pool with both hands, lay on your stomach and kick your feet," the instructor barked.

A couple dozen spindly little white legs began thrashing. "Keep your knees straight," the instructor commanded all of us. What? I couldn't do that. The instructor, safely on the dry edge of the pool and dressed against the cold, walked around inspecting his charges. When he came near me I could see by his face that my kicking wasn't passing muster. "Keep your legs straight," he commanded again. I tried, but it didn't work.

Finally in frustration he pulled off his tee shirt and sweat pants, stripping down to a racing bathing suit, and dove into the pool. Taking two mighty swimming strokes he went half way across the pool and returned to stand next to me. Grabbing one of my legs, he held it so stiff I thought it would break and made me kick straight-legged.

Then he grabbed the other leg and did the same thing. Nodding with satisfaction, he climbed out of the pool, toweled himself off, and made rounds of the other little bodies that were gamely kicking away but getting more tired by the second. By the time he was two steps from me my legs sagged again, back the way they had been before he had gone to all that trouble to hold them stiff.

"OK, that's enough kicking," he yelled, his voice setting off a mightly echo in the glazed brick and tile room. "Now put your back against the side of the pool and stroke with your arms." He stood up high and dry and showed us a stroke we thought would be good enough for him to win the Olympics. Now we tried. The water was stirred up mightily, but a bunch of egg beaters would have done as well.

Eventually, determined to get on with the lesson, he had us stop all the thrashing and put our backs against the wall of the pool. "Now," he barked, "put one foot up behind you and push off from the wall. Put your hands out in front like this." He showed us, bending forward with his huge biceps hugging his ears and arms outstretched.

With a bit of private coaching the kid who had already been recognized as the star pupil demonstrated and floated out to the middle of the pool very easily with his face down in the water. Then another and another tried it with similar success.

My turn came although I kept hoping that the bell would ring before that to end the lesson. Or the building would catch fire. (Oh, that one wouldn't have been too good, we didn't have any clothes on.)

I didn't want to put my face in the water and so held my head up high. That made me arch my back and my neat push off was something like trying to get a beach ball to sail smoothly across the water. I was forced to repeat the exercise, but I was still afraid to put my face in the water. In fact, the instructor finally doped out that my entire problem with swimming was fear of the water, plus weak muscles.

The 10 weeks of lessons continued, and most of the kids became at least passable swimmers, but not me. Apparently my parents got some kind of report of my non-progress and enrolled me for another series of lessons.

I took the course three times before I conquered my fear and got so that I could master some sort of a swimming stroke. I would have been glad to quit at any time along the way, but my parents persisted. I'm glad they did. When I got into Boy Scouts I was able to easily earn merit badges not only in swimming but in lifesaving as well.

I guess if you took swimming lessons at the Y you could enroll in other Saturday classes involving use of the gym. So I presented myself in my little blue gym suit, along with 20 or so likewise nattily attired boys, to Sandy, the gym instructor. What a physique he had for a gray-haired man. We all wanted to look like that.

With his warm personality and Scottish accent he won us over immediately. We'd do anything to please him. Well, in my case almost anything. My spirit was strong, but sometimes my skills and strength left a bit to be desired.

One of his favorite exercises, I suppose to build up the muscles in our arms, was to play catch with a medicine ball. That was a leather ball almost two feet in diameter and heavy. It was all I could do to lift it let alone throw it. But if Sandy wanted me to do it, I'd give it my best shot. I heaved the ball. Whoever was supposed to catch it did and threw it back to me. Ooof. With the aid of my stomach as backstop I caught it and remained standing, but just barely.

We continued like that for a while. Then we were ordered to drag out the gym mats that were rolled up in a corner. We spread them out, and Sandy demonstrated how to do a forward roll. It was what we knew as a somersault. He did it perfectly and sprang lightly to his feet. I thought he must be older than my father but was in the best condition of any man I'd seen off the movie screen.

Now it was our turn. Some of us could do a somersault, but when my turn came I got half way over and flopped sideways. Sandy had all the patience in the world and kept us working at it. Eventually, after many Saturday morning sessions, with Sandy's help, I could do a passable forward roll.

A few of the kids could do handstands, headstands and even backward flips, but I never proceeded to that kind of "graduate work."

Gym sessions ended with a game of soccer, shirts (guys who kept theirs on) against skins (kids who took their shirts off). Sandy refereed with his piercing whistle, but we were more concerned with having fun than following rules, and

Sandy mostly looked the other way at what must have been wholesale violations. We had no idea if there were rules for soccer. Or strategies. All we wanted to do was kick the ball—or each other if we could get away with it.

When I got to gym class in junior and senior high school, what I had learned from Sandy helped, but I was far from an expert in anything. Most things I could make a passable attempt at, but not climbing a rope. The junior high gym had thick ropes that could be lowered from the ceiling, and some kids could climb up them like monkeys. I simply could not pull myself up, not even one foot off the floor. I guess my arms were too weak.

Fortunately there was no Regents examination in rope climbing or anything else in gym class. There were fitness tests, though. I guess they had something to do with the war, which was then going on at full force. The government had been appalled by the number of draftees who were out of shape. So they tried to get schools to work harder at phys ed. My junior high school principal did the *right thing* always and could be depended on to enforce the highest standards the government suggested. If they thought all boys should be able to climb part way up a rope, my principal insisted we go all the way up and upside down too. He'd have met his match with me if he had been the gym teacher. Fortunately for both of us, he wasn't. My instructor just gave up and awarded me a passing score on the fitness tests.

Neither the YMCA nor the public schools in Lockport offered a course in driver education. More's the pity. It would have protected our car from damage and my parents' nerves from unnecessary wear and tear.

My driving lessons were conducted in our spiffy, four-door 1936 dark blue Plymouth sedan. The year by then was 1947.

(Don't look for chronology in these memoirs. My mind doesn't work in strict order. One little memory file drawer opens and spills its contents, then another. The calendar has no effect on them.)

As I said, the year was now 1947. The recent unpleasantness of the Great Depression and World War II were behind us, and gasoline and tires were no longer rationed. New cars were even appearing in showrooms after a long wartime absence. But the 1936 was in good repair and hadn't been driven a lot of miles. It made an excellent classroom.

When the lessons started I was the know-it-all age of 17. I knew how to drive, of course, from watching from the backseat all those years. A lot of the time I'd been moved to the front, mostly when I had become carsick in back. Being up front gave me an action view of the driver, and so I felt very capable of taking the wheel myself. My mother was assigned the job of teaching me, since the lessons were being conducted in the daytime of a summer school vacation, and she and I were home. My father probably thought he had enough frustration with his job, which by then was driving a bus, so he didn't need any more. By 1947 the bakery had long been dead, and even before the end of the war, the machine shop that succeeded it had also gone kaput.

My mother drove out to the edge of town on Beattie Avenue, then a two-lane concrete ribbon going straight nowhere but a perfectly deserted place for a driving lesson.

She shut off the engine, put on the parking brake, and we changed places. There was no fussing with seat belts in those days.

I turned the key and pressed the foot pedal starter. As the car was already warmed up I didn't have to monkey around adjusting the throttle and choke. In cold weather they both had to be pulled out, but just so. Too much and the engine would be flooded with gasoline and wouldn't start. Too little and the starter motor would crank, but the car wouldn't go.

The mighty Plymouth six-cylinder engine was now purring. I tested the accelerator and made it roar. My mother objected so I stopped. I released the hand brake by pressing down on a button on a long lever, and moving the lever forward.

Next I pushed the clutch, the left pedal, to the floor and put the car in first gear. I had studied over and over again a little sketch of the gear pattern, which formed an H. Pull left and down for first, right and up for second, right and down for third. Easy. I pulled left and down and began to release the clutch pedal. The car leaped and stalled. I'd released the clutch too fast.

I shifted back into neutral and started over. The shift lever rose up from the floor of the car by my right foot. I could always tell when it was in neutral because it would wobble freely back and forth. I put down the clutch, shifted into first gear, and tried letting up on the clutch again, slower this time. The car lurched ahead, bounding up and down like a rabbit, but going forward.

Finally it rolled smoothly with the motor roaring as

though it were going to tear itself out of the car. "Shift into second," my mother said, trying to make her voice reflect a calmness she didn't at the moment possess.

I pressed down the clutch again, and the motor roared even louder, but the car slowed down. "Take your foot off the gas a little," my mother counseled, "and shift into second." I did that and let up on the clutch. The car had almost coasted to a stop during this maneuver but apparently had enough momentum so that it could roll on under power again, now in second gear.

More roaring noises, more verbal commands from my mother, and we were soon cruising along at all of 15 miles an hour in third gear. I was driving!

My mother reached over occasionally to correct the steering a little when I seemed headed for a ditch or the wrong side of the road, but we proceeded on. Eventually she relaxed her white-knuckle grip on the dashboard.

After a couple of miles we practiced a right turn and finally stopped and exchanged seats again. The first lesson was over. It had been a triumph of man over machine. Or at least kid over elderly car.

The next day the lesson was repeated, with somewhat less jumping and leaping of the car at the starts but with a dreaded left turn added for increased excitement. Since Beatty Avenue had little traffic, and the cross roads even less, the turn was accomplished very neatly with no danger of a collision.

Over the summer the lessons continued, and I could at last stay on the road without veering into traffic or the ditch. Stops and starts were smoother, and rarely did I now turn a corner sharp enough to cause my mother to scream and grab hold of the door. I'd even driven with my father in the passenger seat and passed muster. He was a professional driver, having lumbered around town with the old bread truck for years and now with busses, with a chauffeur's license to prove it.

Backing up was a bit of a problem, but I'd mastered that well enough, everybody thought, so that I could back the car out of our little one-car garage and down the driveway alone. I was getting pretty cocky.

One day, at lesson time, I flipped the car keys in the air and swung open the garage doors. They didn't roll up as garage doors do now but swung outward on hinges, creating a narrow alley the car had to pass through. No problem. I fired up the mighty engine, put the monster machine in gear, and charged backward out of the garage.

Unfortunately, whoever had driven last (maybe me) hadn't parked perfectly straight or in the center of the garage. As I roared back a fender of the car caught on the edge of one of the wooden garage doors and brought it crashing down on the car. I jammed on the brake and was just getting out of the car when my mother rushed to the scene of the carnage.

The garage door hung dizzily from one of its hinges. Together my mother and I pulled it loose from the car and sort of propped it up so we could get the car out of the way. There were no dents. I was very lucky about that, but there was a great mark of yellow paint where the door had struck. It was the first accident that car had ever been in.

I got a rag and various cleaning agents and scrubbed at the yellow mark, but it was stubborn. Sam Kastner in the paint shop next door would have been able to get it off in seconds, but I wasn't about to approach him. He did peer over the fence and laugh at my plight as soon as he heard the ripping of boards. Eventually the paint rubbed off, or at least enough so that it would show up only under the most exacting examination—my father's.

When he came home he couldn't help but notice the sagging garage door before he came in the house and wanted an explanation. He was not pleased but went out with tools and bolted the poor old door back in its upright position.

A year or so later I was assigned to repaint the garage, and so all traces of the disgraceful affair were expunged. At least I hadn't hung the car up on a rock, as Bob Blount had done with an old model T while roaring around his uncle's farm. It required a tractor to pull the car off the rock, and probably more than one whiskey and soda to calm his father.

My driving lessons continued, but the Door Incident, as it was now known, was never repeated. Before I could get a license I had to know how to make a U turn and parallel park. In Lockport everybody knew where the driving examiners conducted their tests, on a narrow street with a hill, so every student driver went there to practice. Anyone who had moved to that street to enjoy its peace and quiet was sadly disappointed.

The street was too narrow to make a simple U turn, which is why the inspectors chose it. It meant going forward and backward several times to accomplish the turn, I practiced it,

179

looking around very carefully not to hit any parked cars. Those coming up or down the hill couldn't get past, but everybody seemed to know that U-turners were learning to drive and their maneuvers would take a bit of time.

Parking was also practiced on that hill, just to introduce more challenge into the affair. The 1936 Plymouth would look very short next to the cars we now drive, but then parking spaces were smaller, too, so the parallel parking was just as much of a challenge then as now.

The day I went for my test my mother rode with me but then had to get out of the car and let the examiner sit in the front passenger's seat. He was an overstuffed elderly man who must have had an abundance of courage to risk his life several times every day with drivers with scant skills and experience at the wheel.

He asked questions about driving, which I must have answered correctly, then we went for a ride. I stopped oh so carefully at every stop sign and all but got out of the car to look up and down and make sure it was safe to proceed. We went to the practice hill, did the required turn, parked, then went back to his office. He admitted, as though he hated to do it, that I had passed the test and I could go inside and get my license. It was shortly after getting the license that I was allowed to put the Toniusmobile through its paces. My dad rode co-pilot while Tonius slept in the back seat. I still don't know how he could have stayed so calm.

Chapter 12

THE BOY SCOUTS

Wﾛhen my 12th birthday
came around I was eligible to join the Boy Scouts. There was
never any question about which troop I'd sign up with. It
would be Troop 6, which met in the recreation hall of the
Methodist Church. Not only was that my church, the troop
had the reputation of being the best in Lockport in terms of
camping equipment, activities, and leadership.

As soon as I joined I had to assemble all the necessary
paraphernalia, which included the official Boy Scout Handbook and as much of the uniform as my parents could afford
to buy at one time. Boy Scout gear was not cheap, so few of
us had complete uniforms until we'd been in the troop long
enough so that our parents knew we weren't going to drop
out any minute.

The official shirt was heavy khaki, and with it came some

little red badges that my mother had to sew on. They gave the troop number and its hometown. As I advanced I'd get other badges to be sewed on. My mother had to be very precise about the sewing. During our Thursday evening meetings we all had to line up and be inspected by one of the leaders who had seen one too many movies of army top sergeants checking over their men.

Our uniforms had to be pressed just so. Can you imagine a bunch of 12-year-olds and teen-agers keeping their uniforms neat when they had had a wrestling match on the way to the meeting? Badges had to be sewed on straight, with red thread and no sloppy stitches. Even our mothers had to measure up during these inspections.

Pants were supposed to be sharply creased, but the kids who didn't yet have full uniforms had an awful time getting their blue jeans looking presentable. Shoes were a problem, too. We were to wear brown leather shoes and shine them so they'd reflect. We tried, but eventually the inspectors quit looking at shoes. As a matter of fact even our shoes were supposed to be regulation Boy Scout issue, but none were because Scout shoes cost too much.

We learned lots of neat stuff in Scouts, like how to tie a whole bunch of knots, some of them useful to this day, and others good enough to amuse people who never got to be Scouts. I remember being on an airliner once many, many years after being in Scouts when some college students were passing the time by trying to tie various knots. They were miserable at it until my Scout training came to the fore, and I showed them how.

We learned first aid and practiced splinting and bandaging each other. To gain merit badges we not only had to do the bandaging but also describe symptoms and treatment for things from sunstroke to snake bite.

Finally, after all of this spit and polish and learning at the meetings it was time for a game before we went home. Often it was Stone Age football. This required all the proficiency of kick the can and stick ball but none of their rules.

We all took off our shoes, put them in a big pile in the center of the room, and divided into two teams, one at each end of the church recreation hall facing each other. Then the lights were turned off. In the darkness we crept toward the pile of shoes, tried to grab one or two without getting tagged and hurled the shoes at the other team. Sometimes the throws were rewarded with howls of pain as a shoe hit a target in the dark.

When the pile of shoes was gone, we felt around for the shoes that had been thrown at us and fired them back at the enemy. Eventually one of the leaders decided that he really ought to check the battlefield for casualties and see if there was anyone on whom to seriously practice first aid. The lights were turned on and the damage assessed. Everybody seemed to be walking and still having fun. Fortunately the room's windows were covered with stout wire grids, so they escaped the battle unscathed.

The next and most complicated part of the game was finding our own shoes and putting them on. A few sly Scouts had always practiced their knot tying with the shoestrings.

Meetings ended as we all recited the Scout oath, and then we charged out. Next week, same time, maybe a different game.

The highlight of our Scouting was summer camp, two wonderful weeks away from parents, city life, paper routes, and every other vestige of civilization in the ferocious wilds of Allegany State Park. (Proof readers, put away your pencils. The name of the park is really Allegany, not the Pennsylvania-style Allegheny.)

I'd only been a Scout about six weeks when camp time came that first year, and my parents decided that maybe I wasn't ready yet to be that far from home. They sent me instead to the YMCA's Camp Kenan on the shore of Lake Ontario only 25 or 30 miles from home. That way they could get me more easily if I called and told them I was too homesick to stay.

Eventually I learned that Camp Kenan was almost the total opposite of Scout camp. Kenan was professionally organized, sport centered, strict about rules, had archery and rifle shooting, baseball every day, camp uniforms, required recreation and rest periods, had a mess hall big enough to seat everyone in the whole camp. There were paid cooks and counselors, discipline about everything from bed making to where to sit at campfire, and before-breakfast plunges into the ice cubes of Lake Ontario.

Kids who were good at organized sports liked Camp Kenan a lot, but they'd never heard of stick ball, kick the can, or Stone Age football, so I didn't quite fit the mold of the perfect camper.

Assuming that I would go to Scout camp the next summer, I went to the toughening up exercise known as Scout camporee. It should have worked the other way around. After you had been to camp for two weeks every summer for maybe five years you were ready for a weekend camporee. This makes no apparent sense, but I can explain.

Camporee was held on a weekend in early spring and was meant to be a simple camp-out somewhere near Lockport, in some cooperative farmer's orchard or fields. We slept in tents and cooked over open campfires around which we were supposed to sit after dinner and sing trail songs, toast marshmallows, and have a wonderful time. If there had been a camporee brochure, that's the kind of experience it would have described. Unfortunately it wasn't quite like that.

First, the camporee was held on a weekend after at least a full week of rain. The campsite always had some tall grass and looked reasonably dry, but after it had been walked on just once the grass was trodden down into oozing mud. We put up our tents anyway. These tents were little affairs shaped like pieces of pie and not meant for bad weather. In a light breeze or shower our tents could be erected so that the little pointy part faced the wind to protect the big open end.

We held up straws and pieces of grass to test the wind and determined which way to face the tent. There were about seven or eight stakes to be pounded into the ground but the earth was so soft from all the rain that they could be pushed into the mud without benefit of a hammer.

The tent was put up, the stakes pushed in, the single pole shoved tightly into place, and the ropes made taut. All this was done in the rain, of course. But the tent would be dry. Oh, yeah? The ground inside the tent was like a wet sponge. Wherever we crawled (the tents weren't high enough to stand up in) the weight of our bodies brought more water out of the ground. The tents had no floors. We just put down canvas or oilcloth under our sleeping bags. That was supposed to keep out the water.

It was a nice theory but one that never worked. Besides, the wind changed direction every few minutes so that the little pointy end of the tent now faced the wrong way and acted like a funnel to bring the rain inside.

Some of our fathers, mine among them, tried to get a fire going from the wet wood around us. They used quite a few boxes of matches and cans of lighter fluid although that method was contrary to all Boy Scout teaching and strictly forbidden. My father was no kind of outdoorsman, and neither was Clarence Griffin Sr., my best Scout friend's dad. Mr. Griffin had one shoe built up with a two-inch lift and walked with one crutch. You can imagine how much he enjoyed hiking over the rough and muddy ground.

The only one of the dads who really knew something about camping was Sam Weiand, who had all kinds of wood lore or at least led us to think he did. Whenever we asked him a question about how to cope with a camping problem he answered with a couple of winks, nods and sentences we couldn't comprehend.

Eventually the tents got set up, ground cloths were laid, sleeping bags unrolled and a fire started. We each cooked our own food that night, whatever we had brought from home.

The smart kids had brought baloney sandwiches. Those of us who thought we should practice our camp skills tried to cook little steaks, pieces of chicken, or at least hot dogs on sticks over the fire. Everyone's meat fell into the ashes at least once, but we dusted it off and continued cooking. In the end it didn't matter what we had brought to cook. It all tasted like charcoal.

The campfire and jolly songs were cancelled because of the rain, and we crawled into our tents to read soggy comic books by the light of flashlights. Part of the entertainment was also slapping at the mosquitoes.

Finally we went to sleep. That's when the water really began to seep into the tent from all sides and the wind shifted to blow strongly into the open end. We were tough, though; we stuck it out.

The next day, Saturday, we tramped around the wet grounds hunting for Indian arrowheads. In a farmer's apple orchard? Shows how much we knew about Indians or camping or farming. Now and then the rain dwindled to a fine cold drizzle.

To keep up morale one of the leaders tried to organize some sort of game or hike, but mostly they just wanted to huddle around the fire, which they now had whipped up into a respectable blaze. I think somebody had driven to a store during the night for more lighter fluid.

In the early afternoon the scoutmaster, who was younger than our dads but older than the oldest Scout, demonstrated how to cook pot hole beans. In theory you dug a hole and built a fire in it. When the fire had burned down to a thick bed of embers you placed a pot of soaked and boiled beans in the hole and put a cover on the pot. Then you put more hot embers all around the pot and covered the pot and embers with dirt. The pot had a tight cover so the beans wouldn't be contaminated. What you had done was to make a clay oven to bake the beans, and in several hours they could be served piping hot, nicely cooked and seasoned. Nothing would taste better while sitting on a log around a campfire.

That was the theory. It wasn't quite that simple. The hole was dug, but it began to fill with water so had to be bailed out. When it was reasonably dry a bed of sticks was laid down at the bottom, then more were added and set on fire. So far so good, the fire finally blazed. After a while it burned down to very hot embers, just like the scoutmaster had said. He mixed the beans in the pot with a little brown sugar and spices that he'd thoughtfully brought from home, covered the pot, and put it in the hole on the hot embers.

More embers were kicked in from the campfire and dirt was shoved back into the hole and on top of the pot. Perfect. Now he delegated Mr. Griffin and my dad to keep watch and stir the beans once in a while, while all the rest of us went off exploring.

Because of his bad leg, Mr. Griffin was allowed to bring a folding chair to camporee. In fact he had two of them, so he and my dad sat by the bean fire all afternoon. Eventually they decided they should see if the beans were cooking and give them a stir. They carefully scraped off the dirt covering the pot and lifted the lid. It was hot, and they dropped it. That caused some of the piled-up dirt to roll back into the bean pot. Attempts to fish it out with a spoon failed, so they just stirred it in. The beans were brown, the dirt was brown, who would know the difference? The pot was covered again and left to cook some more until it was time to take another look. More dirt sifted into the pot and got stirred in.

When we Scouts and the scoutmaster returned from our maneuvers we sat down to delicious plates of hot beans. My dad and Mr. Griffin were complimented on their fine job, but neither ate much. We assumed that they'd been snacking on the bread and peanut butter or something.

On Sunday morning the sun still refused to shine, and the weather had turned decidedly cold for spring. We broke camp early, much faster than we had set it up, piled into the cars, and went soggily home.

Those with colds were kept home from school the next day, and our mothers were all kept very busy washing muddy clothes and trying to figure out how to get our sleeping bags clean and dry and get rid of the musty smells.

Summer camp could never be that bad. First, we'd be sleeping in cabins with real roofs and floors and shutters that could drop down in case of rain. And July wasn't usually as wet as the spring camporee weekend. Cheered by those thoughts, my parents decided that I was now old enough and experienced enough to venture forth to camp. That summer I went with the troop, riding a school bus for about three hours to reach the southern tier of New York State and the low hills and dense forests of the state park. We lived about six to a cabin, five scouts and a junior leader who was maybe 15 or 16 years old. We ate in our troop's small mess hall and were left pretty much as a troop to plan our own activities. We were assigned swim times by the camp director, but that was just so the lakefront wouldn't be overcrowded. The spit and polish and regimentation of Camp Kenan was far away.

Scout camp did have some discipline, but it was different. Our scoutmaster and Mr. Weiand were the leaders and organized work crews. One crew brought in wood and kept a fire going day and night under a 55-gallon drum that was set on stones over the flames. The drum held water that was kept hot for dishwashing. That "innovation" in camping was so interesting to other Scout leaders that they came around every day to admire the barrel and let out a little water to see how hot it was. It was usually just under boiling temperature.

Another crew of Scouts fetched buckets of water from the tap some distance away and kept the barrel full. Some of us were on KP to help the cooks and to clean up after meals. A couple of Scouts were cooks and once in a while even acted as though they knew what they were doing. One of our junior leaders assigned himself to go to the store every day for whatever supplies the cooks needed. The camp provided an antique wood-paneled station wagon for the five-mile drive to the park store. Every troop sent its own buyer. Prices were outrageous, so we brought as many supplies from Lockport as we could, but we still needed milk and other fresh items.

Tom Foltz, usually called Foo, made the daily trip, which lasted all morning. He got out of the wood and water details and KP that way, could mosey around the store and buy whatever his spending money allowed, and saw girls from other camps who had come in to shop. Foo was about 15 or 16 when he became our quartermaster, so was entitled to be interested in girls.

One more thing appealed to him. Going to the store got him out of sight of his older brother, John, who was the kind of leader who would have been welcomed at Camp Kenan, all discipline and correctness. Foo was neither of those things but very popular with everybody in the troop. In the privacy of our cabins he taught us a few things that were strictly forbidden by the Boy Scout Handbook. I probably shouldn't even mention them, but now, 50 years later, just about everyone who writes a newspaper column of sex advice recommends what Foo taught. The writers have more refined language and can't demonstrate as Foo did, though.

He organized competitions to see how much weight one of our protruding body parts could support if properly encouraged. I think two or three bath towels were usually the limit, but we challenged the champion almost every day to see if we had gained any strength. Foo also taught us how to exercise those body parts by ourselves to prepare us for the sex lives that were sure to come—sometime.

Foo usually also led what we called "initiations." Scouts at camp for their first year had to be inducted with some ceremony. The adult leaders didn't know anything about this, of course, or at least tried not to, but Foo got a few veteran campers together and seized the newcomer, flattened him on his back on a camp cot, and stripped off his shirt. Then

Foo and one other veteran beat a rapid tattoo with their hands on the tenderfoot's bare stomach until it turned pink. This, of course, was called "pink belly." No one ever seemed to get hurt from it, the pain wasn't severe and only lasted a minute or two. And then the tenderfoot who had been initiated realized that he could help initiate others the same way next summer.

Foo had another "initiation" he always talked about but I don't think ever practiced. It gave everybody something to speculate about just the same. How bad would it be? The procedure would have involved treating some tenderfoot's genitals with Sloan's Liniment, an over-the-counter compound sold for relieving sore muscles by making them burn so much you would forget that they were sore.

Foo once even showed us an old bottle of Sloan's, but nobody ever got up the courage to initiate anybody with it. We were all too scared of what damage the liniment would do to the initiatee and what might happen to the initiators when the leaders found out what had happened.

There were other, less painful ways to initiate the newcomers at camp. One was to send them out to look for the "bunk stretcher" or the "sky hook." One of the leaders came out of a cabin one day with a worried look on his face and said, "Frank, we've got a problem in here and need a bunk stretcher to fix it. See if we can borrow one from Troop 8." Off I went on my mission, all filled with pride that I had been selected out of the 20 Scouts to carry out this important task.

At Troop 8's cabins, way across camp from ours, I inquired about the bunk stretcher. Several Scouts and a leader or two seriously discussed where they had seen it last. They'd be only too happy to lend it to us if they could remember where it was. Then someone got an inspiration. "Didn't we lend it to Troop 12?" he asked. They all remembered now, that was exactly where the bunk stretcher had gone.

I marched off to Troop 12, a good distance away, only to learn that they had loaned it to the waterfront director, who had taken it to his family's cabin, which was supposed to be off limits to the Scouts. Well, a duty was a duty. Our leader needed that bunk stretcher, so I dodged lightly over the camp rules and knocked on the waterfront director's cabin door. He said he'd forgive the intrusion because getting a bunk stretcher was urgent business, but he had sent it to Troop 22, which was practicing camping in tents way over across the lake.

After a few more efforts to find the mysterious bunk stretcher I went back to report that I had failed to locate it. Now I could tell by the faces that I'd been off on a wild goose chase. Someone else had been searching the camp for the "sky hook," with an equal lack of success, also because no such implement existed. The joke was repeated year after year, and the newcomers never were any smarter than I was.

At Scout camp all my hard work learning to swim paid off. We not only had swimming every day for fun, but there were also swimming and lifesaving requirements to advance up the ranks, especially to Eagle Scout, the top rank, which I wanted to earn.

We swam in what was called a lake, but was only the size of a pond, although it had a fresh stream feeding it. You could walk around the "lake" in about 10 to 15 minutes if you didn't stay too long at the beaver dam at the far end. Chances are you wouldn't get to see a beaver until evening, and then it would be too dark to find your way around the lake without tripping over a lot of dead logs. Allegany State Park was in the forest primeval. Well, maybe not primeval, since it was mostly second growth after lumberers had been kicked out, but there were big trees, and it was hard walking through the woods because of all the logs that were in various stages of decay, and the soft and mushy moss-covered areas.

The "lake" was cold and clear and had a firm bottom in the shallow end near the swimming area. The waterfront director, who taught swimming, lifesaving, and canoeing, was a young Adonis type. We all thought he was great and what a swimmer and diver. He'd demonstrate a lifesaving dive and come up with every blonde hair of his head in perfect place, a big Pepsodent smile on his face, and not the least bit out of breath after swimming at top speed a couple hundred yards. There were no girls' camps on our lake, so Young Adonis' wife wasn't afraid to let him out of her sight. Their housekeeping cabin was a blissful distance away from all the Scouts.

Under his direction I was able to master the breaststroke, backstroke, and sidestroke, going the proper distances to qualify for my swimming merit badge. Lifesaving was harder. There was a special dive to learn, so that I'd hit the water almost flat and be able to keep my eyes on the make-believe drowning victim who was floundering away a few yards from shore. Then I had to swim the breaststroke so I could continue to keep him in sight, work my way around behind him, and cleverly use leverage to bring his body into a helpless horizontal position to make the "rescue." It took lots of practice, and there was a daily instruction period for all of us who were trying to get our lifesaving badges. Thanks to cooperative drowning victims, who never put up the kind of a fight we were warned that real drowning people would, I passed the course.

Canoeing and rowing were other merit badges I could get at camp if I learned how to paddle a canoe and row a boat and keep them going in straight lines, go the required distances in the allotted time, and do fancy maneuvers like coming up quickly and accurately to land a passenger at a pier. Practice, practice, practice, every afternoon after all the swimmers were out of the water and the coach could go with me for a ride in the canoe or rowboat. Sometimes we'd sneak up near the beavers' house and sit quietly in the water and watch them at work felling trees and building a dam. Finally a beaver would spot us, slap his tail on the water, and dive. That was the last of any beaver watching for that afternoon.

In the evening the coach took his wife out on the lake in the canoe on what would have been a romantic cruise, except for all the Scouts who were watching from the shore and calling out lewd remarks. We were nasty brats.

Hiking was also a big thing for us and involved finding our way through the woods with only a map and compass. Mr. Weiand was a crackerjack at it but wisely held back and let us lead so we'd learn something about reading a map and following compass directions. We learned but walked quite a few extra miles doing it. The popular hiking destinations were an abandoned firewatchers' tower and some huge boulders called Thunder Rocks.

Each destination involved a 14-mile round-trip hike, if we didn't stray, which we always did, but in the end the tower or rocks came into view through a clearing in the trees just in the direction where we had told each other that they would.

There were a couple of other types of hikes, too. These were conducted in the dark. One was the rope hike, which meant that every Scout held onto a rope and tagged along behind the leader. Only the leader had a flashlight. All the rest of us stumbled or got dragged through the woods, over stumps, through brambles and thorns, across swamps, and through brush so that the rope got hopelessly tangled. This procedure was supposed to tire us out so we'd go to bed quietly when it was over. The plan never worked.

There was also the "snipe hunt" in which we went in search of the very rare bird, the snipe, which only came out at night. There really are snipes but the ones we sought were only imaginary. Hunting one required that we sneak through the woods in the dark with no flashlights and keep very quiet so we might hear a snipe's wings beating. We never did. I think the "snipe hunts" were also supposed to tire us out, but they also failed..

We learned a whole lot on the daylight hikes, though— to wear the right shoes *with socks*, to take a full canteen of water and dry matches, maybe lightweight rain gear, to step carefully through the woods, identify poisonous plants and leave them alone. It was good training and I'll bet that

Scouts who became soldiers had a little easier time in basic training.

We cooked our own lunches on the trail, but in camp we had Scouts who had volunteered to be cooks. For two years Clarence Griffin, Jr., and I were the cooks. We carefully planned what we thought would be balanced menus, working several weeks at home on the details and ordering supplies to take along. Since the camp had no electricity, our food had to be kept cold in an icebox, and there wasn't a whole lot of room inside it. That took some planning, but Foo could always get a few things on his daily trip to the store.

We cooked on a two-burner kerosene stove. Maybe it was the stove, or perhaps the high elevation of the camp, but we had a terrible time getting those flames hot enough to boil water. The worst meal we ever had was spaghetti. We needed a big pot of water to cook enough spaghetti to feed 25 Scouts, so we put the water on the stove several hours before dinnertime.

We burned a lot of kerosene, but the water just steamed and refused to boil. It was getting dangerously late, and if we didn't have dinner soon it would be dark and we'd be cooking, eating and cleaning up by flashlight.

Whether the water was boiling or not we had to move on. We dumped a great box of spaghetti into the steaming water and stirred it around. It formed one huge mass of starch that defied anyone to separate it into strings. The sauce came from cans, so it got hot enough over our remaining stove burner, but what good was it on that lump of stuff? We served bread, jelly, peanut butter, and canned fruit in large quantities that night and threw the spaghetti into the garbage.

At Allegany State Park in those days the garbage was collected and dumped at a place where bears could eat it. Their dining room was public, and people sat on bleachers or in their cars and watched them eat. I bet the bears had indigestion that night.

Scouting had a lot to do with learning, and every time we mastered a new skill we could get a merit badge. The top rank was Eagle Scout, attained by getting a lot of merit badges. Most required quite a bit of work.

Griffin (Griff) and I were working together on our merit badges and making good progress but had trouble with the one that required us to identify a given number of birds. We were trying to do it in late fall when most of the birds had departed from Lockport. We made many trips before sunrise to various places where there should have been lots of birds and finally managed to record enough to get the merit badge.

Fire building was our last hurdle. There are several ways to start a fire without matches. The smart asses in the troop told us to use cigarette lighters, but we knew that wouldn't do at all. We could hit flint and steel together to get sparks which we would fan to life, or we could spin a stick round and round against a board so that the resulting friction would heat some kind of tinder until it flamed.

We tried both methods and failed over and over again. Still, we wanted to be Eagle Scouts, and this fire-building challenge was in our way. We hit steel against flint time after time, but the sparks just went out. The spinning stick got hot, but the tinder didn't catch fire. We tried every kind of tinder we could gather up. I thought maybe that's what Thomas Edison went through as he tried every material in creation to get one that would glow in his light bulb.

Finally a spark caused a little glow in the tinder. We blew on it oh so gently, and miracle of miracles, it grew into a tiny flame. We added the thinnest and driest of sticks one at a time. They flamed too, so we ventured to try a bit larger ones. At last we had what anyone would recognize as a fire. And we had witnesses, too, our troop leaders who were as overjoyed as we were to think that Troop 6 would now have two more Eagles. I still have the newspaper photo noting our achievement.

Chapter 13

THE WORLD OF WORK

Even though school didn't end until 4 o'clock, activities took place afterward. There were sports, of course, and some clubs, but I never got into them because by then I was in business for myself. OK, it was only delivering newspapers, but, as the paper reminded us now and then, we were our own bosses. Except that it decided what time of day we'd start and end our deliveries, which houses we'd deliver to, how much we'd charge for the papers, what we'd have to pay for our papers, when we had to pay our bills, and we'd have to arrange for our own substitutes if we wanted to take a vacation or day off. Besides those few things we were on our own.

I delivered the *Buffalo Evening News* to an enlightened group of customers who were interested in learning more about what was going on in the world that they'd ever know by reading just the local *Union-Sun & Journal*. There were always a few people, thank goodness, who wanted to know about doings in Washington, not just what the ladies of the First Baptist Church of Lockport were going to serve at their fall luncheon. If anything happened in Lockport, it was a column of news for the *Union-Sun & Journal.* Anything that had occurred somewhere else was lucky to merit a single paragraph.

My *Buffalo Evening News* route went up Pine Street, almost from downtown to the city line. The Pine Street Gang was gone, so nothing bothered me except the snow and cold, especially when I went around what I called "The Horn," the far end of the route. I only had about 50 papers to deliver in all that long distance. The *Union-Sun* had two or three routes in my territory because they served almost every house. The *Union-Sun* usually contained only about 24 pages. The *News* was often 60 or more pages thick, which is why I needed a bicycle with a stout basket to carry the papers even when I had to plow through snow.

Papers were delivered by truck from Buffalo about 2 p.m. every day to a little brick building on an alley not far from the high school. The place might have been a blacksmith's shop once, or maybe an auto repair garage. It had very little light and no regular heat. There was a furnace in which the surplus papers and the wrappers from the bundles were burned for a few moments of warmth. I'd arrive at the little building about 10 minutes after four and have to double check while the distributor, Sterling Kolb, or his wife counted out my papers. They counted them like lightning and never made a mistake.

I don't know what I would have said if I'd thought I was being cheated. I dated their daughter, Mary, once in a while, including the senior prom.

It took an hour or more to make my deliveries, longer on Fridays when I tried to collect money from each customer. Those I couldn't find home I went back to see on Saturday, and if all else failed after a few more attempts I left a note threatening to stop delivery of their paper. That fixed them. Most customers apologized and paid up the 20 or 25 cents a week they owed for six-day delivery.

My favorite customer was one I called "the blue man." His skin was actually blue, which I thought quite a mystery. I still do, except that a cardiologist once told me about a heart drug that turns the skin blue permanently if the patient goes out in the sun.

"The blue man" was a skinny little fellow, maybe 30, who lived in a second floor apartment. When I went to collect I hoped he wouldn't come to the door. I wanted to see his wife. She was a dish, not a blue plate either. What's more, she scratched the palm of my hand as she put the quarter in it.

Blount said that was an invitation to have sex with her, but I never managed it. I didn't even know how to suggest it and certainly wouldn't have known how to perform it. I was only 12 years old.

I started to deliver papers when I was still at Emmett Belknap and kept the route through my junior year of high school, making me the longest tenured carrier on the force. Much good it did me. There were no bonuses. All of us paperboys did threaten to go on strike once for a bigger share of the collections. Mr. Kolb finally said we could raise the price of the paper by three cents a week and keep the three cents. That was $1.50 and meant something. The strike threat ended.

I also had another job, if you could call it that. When I was about 10 or 11 years old Mrs. Ranney, who lived next to Donners, beckoned to me from her porch one day. I was scared of her, as we all were on Waterman Street, but I approached. She asked me if I would set her garbage pail out to the curb for collection. She'd pay me a quarter. That was easy money, so I did it. That led to other requests, this little chore, that little job, change a light bulb, take a coat down from a high hook and hang it somewhere else. One thing after another, every day that summer. Sometimes she called just as we were getting ready to go somewhere, and it wasn't convenient to run over to her house. I went, though, because she got mad if I didn't. And she had started to pay more—50 cents and a dollar to do a few minutes of work. Finally she got too insistent on my time, and I told her that I couldn't help her any more. It was years before I realized that she was just lonely and had no friends or relatives. How pitiful that she had to look to a kid for friendship and then picked one who didn't even realize how hungry she was for the sound of a voice that didn't come from the radio.

During my senior year in high school I was offered a new job working in George Pool's grocery store on Pine Street. We did most of our shopping at Pool's when the little Waterman Street store was between owners, as it so often was. George Pool's tiny Red and White Store (that's what its "brand" was, as well as its colors) kept running year after year maybe because Pine Street had more traffic than Waterman did. The traffic was good for the store but not for the Pine Street kids, who had to find other places to play kick the can and go slamming.

I leaped at George's job offer. (He was always George and never Mr. Pool.) I could work after school and all day Saturday, the store was near home, and the pay was good—35 cents an hour plus an occasional piece of penny candy or handful of pretzels from the bulk container, but only if there were no customers in the store. I'd had the paper route for five years, and it was time to move on. Besides I'd gotten nowhere with the blue man's wife.

George's store was in the front room of what had once been a long narrow house. You walked up about six steps to a wooden porch and then entered a room about 12 feet wide by 20 or 25 feet deep with shelves on two sides, a meat refrigerator across the back, a counter down the center, and several bushel baskets full of squash, potatoes and such along one side where they were always in the way of clerks and customers. The store was so small that there was no place for them, and George, who read *Modern Grocer Magazine* every month, knew that people bought more if they couldn't avoid seeing the merchandise. Or in his case, tripping over it.

Under the porch was a door about three feet high leading down a few stairs to a dank and musty cellar where boxes of canned goods, 100-pound sacks of potatoes, cases of pop and other items that wouldn't be hurt by dampness were stored.

Out in back of the store, in what had once been a two-car garage, were eight-foot-high stacks of boxes containing cereals, paper products, candy, sugar, flour, everything packed in paper or cardboard that couldn't tolerate the dampness of the cellar but could stand the cold of the unheated garage, which George always referred to as the warehouse.

One of my jobs was to keep the little store's shelves stocked with items from the cellar and warehouse. George looked around the shop every afternoon and wrote down on narrow sheets of cardboard everything that was lacking on the shelves. He saved the cardboard from boxes of shredded wheat; they were the little dividers between the biscuits. George never wasted anything.

He'd write 2 RW tom pas, 1 cs CC, 4 DM wh kn co and on and on down several cards. By the way, the translation of those items is two cans of Red and White brand tomato paste, one case Coca-Cola and four cans of Del Monte whole kernel corn. It was often a challenge to figure out the list.

There was only room for six cans in a row on each shelf, so there was constant running up and down steps to the cellar to replenish the stock. Getting things from the warehouse was a bit more challenging. It meant a trip outside, around the store, opening the overhead garage door, and maybe moving box after box to get to one buried at the bottom of a high stack. George refused to sell beer, so I was spared hauling those bottles and cans out of the basement, but that was about the only place he drew the line. He tried to have a little of everything, even a few cuts of meat that he really didn't keep on hand but got from a larger Red and White store for customers who ordered them.

Tuesday was freight day. When I showed up after school the front porch of the store was stacked six or eight feet high with corrugated boxes of merchandise to be put in the cellar or warehouse. The store closed at nine, but I usually worked only a few hours on school days. Tuesday, though, I knew I might have to stay later, until everything was neatly put away.

While I was doing that I also had to restock shelves and wait on customers if more than one showed up in the store at a time. There really wasn't room for more than two customers and a clerk or two.

Saturday was another busy day. I worked at least from 9 to 5, and if George was going out, stayed and closed up at 9 that night. Saturday was when many of our regular customers shopped by phone. George took the calls while I waited on the walk-ins, or the reverse. On Saturday we also had an extra clerk for a few hours, and we were all busy.

In whatever lulls there were between customers we had to pack the phone-ordered groceries into boxes. Things that needed to stay cold were wrapped and left in the refrigerator, but a note was put into the box. The boxes were lined up along one side of the store where everybody had to trip over them, but again, there was no other space.

About two o'clock George loaded the first batch of boxes in his car to make deliveries, stopping first at a bigger Red & White Store, owned by a friend of his, to pick up the cuts of meat that had been ordered. On his way out the door with the orders George always said, "Frank, this store needs a damn good dusting."That was his one word of profanity and if Mrs. Pool had heard it George would have been chastised. All he was trying to say was that I should dust everything in between refilling the shelves after our busy morning, and take care of the afternoon customers as well.

When I say take care of them, that's what I mean. There was no self-service. Everyone stood at the little counter and told George or me what they wanted, one item at a time. We'd get it and put it on one end of the counter, then the next item and the next. Eggs had to be counted out into paper bags behind the refrigerator, which was called the meat case.

Cold cuts and cheese had to be sliced on the big danger-ous-looking electric slicer, just as much as each customer wanted, and then wrapped.

Vegetables from the bins and baskets were put into paper bags and weighed while the customer watched to make sure we didn't slip in a potato that was soft or an onion that had sprouted. Bananas were cut from a big bunch on order with a long hooked knife.

When everything was assembled its price was written down in pencil on a brown paper bag, then the figures were added. There was no adding machine. George could look at a column of figures and come up with a total in seconds. It took me considerably longer, adding first up from the bot-tom, then down from the top. If the two answers didn't agree it all had to be done again until they did.

Everything was then packed in paper bags or boxes, mak-ing sure that the fragile things including the eggs in their bag, weren't crushed. When the customer forked over money (never any checks) I went to the cash register on the end of the counter and pushed down the appropriate keys, maybe two or three at one time. To ring up $2.85 you had to push the $2 key, the 80-cent and the 5 cent all at once. Then the cash drawer would pop open. The machine was not electric but was all decorated with ornate gold carvings. It was more of a work of art than a business device, but when keys were pushed little numbers popped up mechanically in the window on top, a bell rang and the cash drawer opened. It took quite a bit of strength to push down the keys, as well as big hands to reach them all at the same time. It didn't add up the purchases and it certainly didn't calculate change.

The highest amount of money that could be recorded on the register was $2, so a sale of $10 meant pushing down the $2 five times consecutively. Customers seemed happy to wait during all this procedure. George was a master of small talk and managed also to call their attention to some of the advertised specials for the week or a few things that were tucked away out of sight because there was no way to keep all of the stock out where people could see it, although he tried. The counter was so covered with things on sale that there sometimes wasn't space to put the customer's order. A big order in those days was about 10 or 12 items. Anything more than that would overload the counter and make the addition process exceedingly long if I had to do it.

George taught me that customers would often buy things they hadn't intended to. That was why he tried to keep as may items as possible on the counter even if it did mean giving up workspace. We encouraged customers to overspend in several ways. For instance, when someone wanted a pound of sliced baloney I'd cut off one slice, hold it up so they could determine whether the thickness was right, then slice away on the electric machine. I'd put a piece of paper on the scales and put the slices on. "Oops, that's a pound and two ounces," I'd say. "Shall I take some off?"

The customer would almost always say, "Oh, no, that's all right." George was sly, but never dishonest. His church wouldn't have let him even think about cheating.

George counseled me, "If you cut too much you sell two or three extra pounds every week." It was even easier with the liver sausage, which was too soft to slice on the machine and had to be sold as a chunk, cut off from the long sausage with a knife. I'd estimate what a one-pound chunk was and cut it off. What do you know? I'd cut too much, but the customer would buy it anyway. More extra money went into the till. I treated the store as though it were my own, even if my share was only 35 cents an hour.

I also had to learn some tricks about closing at nine o'clock. First, I'd go out to the front porch and look both ways. If anyone was in sight and headed my way I'd stay open until I could see if they were coming into the shop. If not, I'd quickly lock the door and pull the chains to turn out each of the front lights. Then I'd run to the back and switch off the central overhead light, leaving on only the light in the meat refrigerator case so I could find my way around.

Then big sheets of butcher paper had to be placed neatly over all the meat and cheese in the case. The fresh fruit and vegetables that were sitting out in baskets had to be put away in the lower part of the refrigerator, next to the milk. When that was done I could switch off the light in the meat case and grope my way to the front door, go out and test it to make sure that it had locked behind me. Next I had to lock the padlock on the cellar door from the outside and go around to the garage and test the lock there. The money had been left in the cash register for George, who would take it out when he got home, stuff it into an empty coffee can and hide the can somewhere in the family living quarters, which were behind and above the store.

I enjoyed the grocery business so much I continued to work there the summer after I graduated from high school, and the summer after my first year at Alfred University. By now I was one of the family, chatting with Mrs. Pool and their two daughters, both of whom were a few years younger than me.

One Saturday night, after locking up, Blount and I intended to go out and have a big time. That meant going to a sleazy run-down bar near the old railroad station and drink a beer. After our somewhat shaky start at drinking we had by now gained the ability to down a glass of beer without throwing it up.

The main business of the excursion to the bar, however, was to listen to any railroad gossip we could overhear. We'd keep one ear cocked for the sound of an approaching train. There never were any, and the railroad gossip sounded more like factory workers' talk about hunting and fishing.

There never were more than four or five people in the bar, counting the bartender, on Saturday nights. Apparently the bar, like the railroad, had dwindled almost to oblivion.

From previous visits Blount and I knew that while the beer was decently priced, the little bags of pretzels and potato chips that they sold were far too expensive for us. I was working in a store where I could buy a great big pound bag of pretzels cheaper than the price of one of the dinky ones in the bar. Why not take a big bag of pretzels from the store and eat them in the bar along with our beer?

It seemed like an excellent plan, so I weighed out a big bag full and put the money in the cash register before we left for the bar. When the store locking up procedure was finished we set off for Lockport's version of Grand Central Station in Blount's dad's car.

After getting a beer apiece and settling ourselves at one of the 20 or so vacant tables, we discovered that we were more or less the center of attention from the regulars at the bar. "What the hell do them two school kids want in here?" they asked each other and shook their heads.

With everyone watching us, we decided that we ought to be rather circumspect about getting the pretzels out of the bag. We put it on the floor where it might not be noticed in the gloom of the bar and sneaked the pretzels out and into our mouths one at a time. After one beer we'd had enough of this subterfuge and decided that the train wasn't going to arrive that night after all, and we left.

Although I liked working in the store during the summer after my freshman year of college, I decided that the next summer I'd like to earn more money, and George Pool wasn't able to pay it. Besides, now I could use the family car to get to a more remote job, since my dad never drove it to work. I hunted through ads in the *Union-Sun & Journal* and came across one for summer help at a basket factory.

It was an ancient-looking low stone building nestled on the bank of the canal in Lowertown. It had no sign on the side facing the canal and Market Street, where all the traffic was, but around in back there was a little legend that proclaimed that the business of the establishment was the manufacture of fruit baskets. I'd never thought of it before, but Lockport was in the center of the Niagara County fruit belt and somebody had to make bushel and half-bushel baskets to put that fruit in.

I was hired at the magnificent sum of 57½ cents an hour to help make covers for bushel baskets. The covers were formatted and stapled together by two girls. (I suppose we have to say women now, but they called themselves girls.) They handed each cover as they made it to a blind man who worked next to me. He added two little wire fastening tabs to the cover and passed it to me. I stacked and tied the covers in bundles of 12 and put them on a cart to be taken up to the top of the factory where they were dried in an oven. It was boring work, and the only thing that made the days pass was the banter that went on between all of us. You had to be broad-minded.

Once I was sent to the department where whole logs were cooked in hot water to loosen their bark. After they had been in the water long enough my job was to hook them with a chain hoist so they could be lifted out of the vat. Sometimes I had to walk across the vat of nearly boiling water on little cement or board catwalks. It was dangerous and I didn't like it, so was glad when I was put back on my easier job. Later that year I read in the paper that someone had fallen in the vat and been scalded to death.

One summer in the basket factory was enough. I decided right then that I wanted no part of any manufacturing job, ever. The next summer I worked for the City of Lockport Street Department. My dad knew Pete Loomis, superintendent of streets, who lived near Tonius, so he asked Pete to hire me for the summer. The job I got must have been a political plum; I was the only person hired for the summer.

What was it about Lockport? Pete's name wasn't Pete, it was Ralph. Tonius wasn't Tonius, Hugo wasn't Hugo, and Greasy wasn't Greasy. Confusion reigned.

Pete assigned me to a crew of four headed by a guy named Criswell, who was the driver of the truck, which made him our boss. Every day Pete gave Criswell our work assignment. Sometimes we took some blacktop and a few tools and patched holes in the street. Other times we drove around the city and picked up piles of brush that people had cut down and left in front of their houses.

Once in a while we were part of an all-out assault to pave a street. Criswell was assigned to go to the blacktop plant and bring the blacktop. The rest of us shoveled up loose stones, chipped away at the curbs or did whatever else we could to look busy. Pete knew nothing about paving streets and turned the job over a serious little man named Rosie, who gave us all orders. When Criswell had dumped the hot blacktop into the newly dug out street Rosie became General Patton and ordered everyone, including Pete, into battle with rakes and shovels to smooth out the new street. How fussy he was. You'd have thought he was installing a dance floor.

The day after we'd put in a new street we'd get an easy job. Pete was tired out from doing his few minutes of raking and then leaning on the rake for the rest of the day watching Rosie create order out of chaos. The next day we'd go back to picking up brush, which mostly meant that we just sat in the truck and cruised around the city at 10 miles an hour. We always had to look busy or else people might complain to the mayor about us wasting taxpayers' money, and Pete would be in trouble.

On Saturdays we were usually assigned to pick up garbage. Criswell drove a dump truck, not a modern vehicle that is easy to load and compresses the garbage. I walked along one side of the street, a buddy went along the other, and we pitched the full garbage cans up over the side of the truck to Hod, who worked up on top, emptying the garbage cans and neatly stacking the contents into a nice pyramid so that the truck could carry a large load.

"Look at Hod," Criswell said every Saturday, "look how old he is and is still working. He makes an art of stacking up the garbage. Nothing ever falls off the pile when Hod stacks it."

We all agreed that Hod was an expert at his job and we certainly weren't qualified to fill his high rubber boots and wade around in the garbage. He was stone deaf, so we never were able to tell him that we admired him. Even if your job is menial, when you do it well "Attention must be paid," as Willy Loman's wife said.

The "atmosphere" on the garbage truck may not have been the sweetest, but the pay was sure better than I had gotten in the grocery store or the basket factory. I think it was close to a dollar an hour. What I saved during the summer went a long way toward buying college books in the fall.

Chapter 14

OFF TO COLLEGE

As you gathered, high school ended for me, "not with a bang, but a whimper," or to be more accurate, throwing up in the bushes with Bob Blount after graduation. After the summer at George Pool's grocery store it was off to Alfred University for four years. You never heard of Alfred University and don't know where it is?

If you read the annual list of the best American small colleges in *U.S. News and World Report*, you'll find Alfred among them. It is a small university in Western New York State. If you draw a line on a map south from Rochester and stop just before you get to the Pennsylvania border, you should be somewhere around Alfred, which, according to the Alma Mater "is the pioneer college of Western New York." When I was there the song continued "Alfred, the mother of men." That bit got changed later, so at alumni reunions some of us are singing "mother of men" and others have different words.

I wanted to go to a small college. Alfred wasn't my first choice, Bates College in Maine had that honor. I'd gone with my folks on a vacation when I was maybe six years old through Maine, but that wasn't why I wanted to go to college there. I just liked their brochure. But the cost of getting to Maine and home every year, and on Christmas and Easter vacations as well, would have been prohibitive. So Alfred it was, especially since it offered a small scholarship.

My folks and I went down to look Alfred over and meet the lady who handled admissions. She had an office upstairs in a building grandly known as The Green Block but which obviously had started its life, many years earlier, as a group of small stores on Alfred's Main Street.

The counselor was a young woman with a soft southern accent who seemed to have all the time in the world. As we entered the office she quickly kicked a bunch of empty Coke bottles deeper under her desk where she thought we might not notice them and began describing Alfred, the curriculum, the campus life, etc. Then we went on a little tour during which she said "hello" to everyone we met and they said "hello" to her. It was a campus custom, she explained. Everybody greeted everybody.

The university buildings were a collection of old and new structures in a wooded glen, and sure enough, as the Alma Mater said, the babbling brook ran along through the campus and it was all "beneath the sheltering pines." I somehow felt as though I already belonged there.

In the fall my folks moved me into Bartlett Dormitory, the dorm for freshmen men. It was a broad two-story red brick building with tall Grecian white pillars and had comfortable single and double rooms. Mine was a double, shared with Bob Sheehan, a student I'd never met. In the middle of the year he moved into a fraternity house or another room, and I ended up with the big double room to myself. It looked out onto Pine Hill, which rose up to isolate the campus from the woods behind it. Pine Hill was supposed to be the spot for romantic encounters, but with Alfred's severe snowy winters and wet springs, I doubt if the hill saw as much fooling around as everyone wanted to believe.

I blamed the hill for ruining the reception on my little portable radio, and everyone in the dorm had the same problem. We got only a tiny station in Hornell, about 20 miles away, during the daytime. (The station went off the air at sunset.) Once in a while I could hear a raspy whisper from a station in Rochester but not often and not clearly. I didn't have time to listen to the radio anyway.

Freshmen were obliged to wear little green beanie caps for the first semester. The idea was that all lost souls could recognize each other and get acquainted and that upperclassmen would be tolerant. My first impressions of the campus proved to be accurate; the place was very friendly, professors were approachable and could often be found shooting the bull with a group of students in the campus center, or Student Union, as it was known then. There was no such thing as a "teaching assistant." Profs did their own work; most were Ph.D.'s, and being a department chairman didn't excuse them from having an open door to students.

The only formality in the dorm was at dinner. All meals were sit-down affairs served by students who got free meals by waiting on tables. Dinner required us to wear coats and ties. One of us (the honor/duty rotated) had to take Mrs. Smallback, the housemother, by the arm and lead the procession to the dining room. Alfred did its best to civilize us.

Freshman girls lived at a dormitory called The Brick near the center of the campus. It had a somewhat larger dining room than the one at Bartlett, so some students who didn't live at The Brick also ate their meals there. The same rules of "dressing for dinner" applied. Girls wore skirts, no slacks, puleeze. Student waitresses wore blue uniforms (the head waitress wore white), and the waiters had white jackets.

The housemother there was escorted "down" to dinner, since the dining room was on the basement level. Her duties were somewhat more onerous than Mrs. Smallback's at Bartlett. She had to be in the lobby at curfew to see that the girls were in on time, and all boys were then swept out of the lounge. Curfew was 10 o'clock on weeknights, 11 on weekends, and sometimes as late as midnight for special events. Girls who were late a couple of times were "campused," meaning that they weren't allowed outside the building after dinner for a given number of evenings. Maybe they could get permission to go to the library, but I don't think there was any notion of stopping in the Student Union.

The 8 a.m. class three days a week met in venerable old Kenyon Hall for a course called Civilization, an overview of literature, art, world history, philosophy, and a dollop of whatever else would introduce us to studying in college style. The class was about the only time that the freshmen from the College of Ceramics had a class with those of us in the College of Liberal Arts, away from their smelly chemistry and dusty ceramics.

Prof. "Dutchy" Barnard kicked off the program with general lectures and often wound up reciting poems in his singsong voice. A year later when the administration eased him out of his job (we never did learn why) all of us in the English Department were up in arms, but it didn't do any good. He went gracefully. Taking his place was Mel Bernstein. Oh, my God, Alfred had hired a Jew, its first ever!

As it turned out Mel was the best teacher in the Liberal Arts program. That was not just my opinion but came from the whole college. He was elected to every academic leadership office the college had, became "Mr. Alfred," and even served as mayor of the village, a triumph in a village of right-wing Republicans from a tiny ultra-conservative religious denomination.

Alfred was full of excellent teachers. Willis Russell, who taught history, could never bring himself to criticize anyone. His lectures included such statements as, "Now you take that fellow Mussolini. He thought he was doing the right thing trying to get Italy on its feet, and he didn't know that that other fellow, Mr. Hitler, would turn out to be so rotten. You can't really blame old Mussolini for the way things turned out."

Fred Engleman, professor of political science, was ever smiling and ever cynical. He had us read books about why political machines sometimes provided better government than bumbling do-gooders. Engleman was also fun as a friend. One spring day he was walking through the campus with Dan Pierotti, a classmate and pal of mine, the two of them discoursing learnedly. Suddenly Dan looked around, and the professor was missing. He was face down in a bed of hyacinths. "I just love the smell of hyacinths" was the only excuse the learned professor offered.

In the English Department Leila Tupper had the reputation of being a tyrant. A tiny lady of a certain age, she had a talent for posing nearly unanswerable questions and demanding answers. Everybody was afraid of her—except my buddy Dan Pierotti, of hyacinth fame. He got the notion that a few students should form a club to read plays aloud, each of us taking a part. We needed a faculty member, but why on earth did he pick Leila Tupper?

As it turned out we all had a ball. She invited our group to meet in her cozy apartment over a garage where we read plays and shared tea. Dan picked the plays, Restoration comedies that were as naughty as could be. Leila, of course, was always selected to read the bawdiest part and loved it. I learned that a gruff exterior is sometimes only skin deep.

After my success with math in high school I intended to major in it in college. A big mistake. There was a large gap between high school and college math and I couldn't find a bridge over it. One semester of calculus was enough. All I remember from the class is how Prof. Nevins began in the fall. He came in wearing a felt hat which he kept on for a few minutes while he drew a large hook on the blackboard. Then he took off his hat and slapped it onto the blackboard over the drawn hook. The hat stayed. Nevins had carefully positioned his drawn hook at the very spot where he had hammered in a tiny nail earlier which we couldn't see. The hat stayed on the board "by magic," and that was only the beginning of the math mysteries that Prof. Nevins tried to unwrap. All the rest proved to be beyond my comprehension.

Nevins also ran the three-times-a-week movies in Alumni Hall, for which he charged 25 cents admission. They were a cheap date. His wife sold the tickets and Nevins himself made slides that preceded each film, things like "Ladies are requested to remove their heads."

Up the hill from Alumni Hall was a carillon played by Ray Wingate every Sunday afternoon and on some other occasions like Homecoming weekend. My friend Matt Melko was not a fan of what he called "those damn bells," so managed to get the number of the telephone up in the little cabin high up in the carillon tower where Prof. Wingate banged the levers to ring the bells. Melko phoned right after the music started. Dr. Wingate quit playing to answer the phone. No one there. He began again, and within a minute or so the phone rang again. He'd stop playing to answer, but still no one. I don't know how long this would have continued, but eventually the phone was disconnected.

Melko and I spent more time than we should have working on the campus weekly newspaper, called the *Fiat Lux*, named for the university's motto, which means in Latin, "Let there be light." Our news columns covered everything happening on the campus, at least everything we could find out about that was, as *The New York Times* says, "fit to print." I'm not sure that our editorials shed much light, but we got all heated up over a variety of things.

Matt and I thought the university registrar, Clifford Potter, was a stuffed shirt who did little to improve the efficiency of his office. My friend Dan Pierotti, always a troublemaker despite his intention to go into the ministry, and I found a telephone pole on the ground. The Alfred telephone company (an independent, two-person firm) was going to install the pole if it ever got around to it. Since the registrar's office was also the office for lost and found articles, we delivered the pole there, stating that we had found it. We left the pole partly inside the registrar's office, partly out in the hall. They couldn't close the door to go out for lunch. Dan and I disappeared very quickly after leaving the pole. The clerks in the office were too startled to see who we were.

The next week's *Fiat Lux* carried an article about the caper, not naming the culprits, but saying that "Registrar Potter professed to be ignorant." No mention of what he was ignorant about. He probably had better sense than to read the *Fiat*, so we never heard anything from him.

Freedom of the press was wonderful. Matt and I did push it beyond its boundaries, though. We took some strong editorial stands, about things of consequence and of no consequence. Our motto, as stated in the yearbook, was "The *Fiat Lux*, like all good newspapers, prints the news and raises hell."

One December day there appeared on campus a single sheet handbill attacking the *Fiat*. The handbills were posted and dumped all over town, in the Student Union, in fraternities, sororities and dormitories, in the president's office, everywhere. A meeting of the Student Senate was even interrupted by the appearance of Santa Claus in full regalia, who dumped a big pile of the handbills on the senators' meeting table.

No one ever learned who published and distributed the scurrilous paper, called the *Rebel*. Its masthead said it came from the Leber Institute. Careful readers might have ascertained that Leber was *Rebel* spelled backward. Matt and I were the editors and distributors. This is the first time this information has *ever* been made public. I thought I made quite a dashing appearance in that Santa Claus suit.

We took the precaution of typing the *Rebel* at a place where no one could interrupt us and see what we were doing. The perfect place to work was the office of the university's public relations director. As editors of the *Fiat Lux*, we had keys to his office.

There were some other notable pranks. The village clock, in a high tower, mysteriously stopped one night when Dan Pierotti and I jammed something in its gears. The absence of its quarter-hour bells eventually brought a maintenance man who got the clock going again.

Then there was the day that I stole a police car— the Village of Alfred's only one—and moved it around the corner. When interviewed later by a *Fiat Lux* reporter (me), the policeman—also Alfred's only one—confessed that it had been a bit of poor judgement to leave his keys in the car.

There were other troublemakers on campus besides Melko, Pierotti, and me. One was even on the faculty, Prof.

Galway Kinnell, who taught English. I thought he was a great guy and twice even attended three-week summer programs to take his courses. We met outside under a tree and read and talked about poetry in the mornings. Afternoons and evenings were free, and there was no homework. Our amusement was watching the ceramic engineering students who were required to take the short summer session to learn surveying. Every year the campus was surveyed, and every year the buildings had moved again. No one ever figured it out.

Galway Kinnell looked like a rugged young boxer. He needed a woman to remind him to get a haircut once in a while and to send his coat to the cleaners, something he never thought of doing. He probably thought he needed a woman for something more interesting, and I think arranged that with one of his students. He lived in one of the pre-fabricated buildings that had been thrown together just after the war to house married veterans.

Galway did a very naughty thing by conducting one of his poetry seminars in his apartment. Strictly against Alfred's rules! Yes, Lelia Tupper had students in her apartment, but she was an old woman. Galway was a young, virile and attractive stud. He broke another rule by serving beer during the seminars. Could anything have been worse in Alfred?

The Village of Alfred and the university were "dry," which meant no alcoholic beverages of any kind were to be sold or served. Fraternities skated around the rule, of course, at their parties, and that seemed to be OK, but for a Learned

Professor to serve beer! Well, it probably was grounds for dismissal. As a matter of fact, Galway only stayed a couple of years. Since then he has become a noted poet and published several books of poetry. His biography makes no mention of Alfred, but I had the nerve to invite him to return for an alumni reunion. He didn't come but wrote me and said that although he hadn't been fond of Alfred, he somehow felt "fully alive" while there.

Alcohol was forbidden because the university was founded by the Seventh Day Baptist Church, a little denomination that has all but disappeared. Stores closed at sundown Fridays and remained closed until sundown Saturday. That was the sabbath, when the SDB's, as they were called, went to church. The non-SDB's used the same church building on Sundays, so that was convenient. Alfred had the unusual distinction of having its post office and bank closed Saturday and open Sunday.

The problem arose with football games, which were not played on Saturday afternoons. The university had left SDB control many years earlier but didn't want to offend the majority population of the village, so football was played Saturday night, never in the afternoon.

That sometimes let to amusing (or unfortunate, as you will) consequences. The weather at night in the fall could be downright cold in Alfred. And I remember one notable game in which fog rolled in so thick that neither players, referees, nor fans knew what was happening on the playing field. I had to phone the news wire services after the game with the score and a paragraph describing a couple of the best plays. I really had no clue what had happened. My paragraph was about the fog and the officials' best guess about who might have scored.

Professor Nevins didn't flout the SDBs but did run his movies on Friday evenings. That must have been OK, since they were shown inside a university building that had no movie-type marquee and there was no advertising except a conservative poster in the lobby of Alumni Hall, where the movies were shown. And besides, no one could dislike Professor Nevins. It was his darned math that was the problem.

In my junior and senior years I became the university and village correspondent for several newspapers and news wire services. In addition to the football scores, I sent them stories about university news and long play-by-play reports of the thrilling meetings of the village Board of Trustees. The stories were long because I got paid 10 cents per inch for whatever was printed, and at least the *Wellsville Reporter* used the stories almost full length. It helped that the editor was an Alfred alumnus who graduated two years before I did and had also been the university and village correspondent.

Every month I got a small check from each of the newspapers and wire services I served. It was just a few bucks, but made me feel that I was really working in the big leagues when I got paid by the Associated Press, United Press, the old International News Service, and papers like the *Buffalo Evening News, Rochester Democrat & Chronicle* and papers in the smaller cities of Hornell, Wellsville, Olean, and Elmira.

During my last three years of college I earned my meals by working as the dishwasher in The Brick dormitory's kitchen. What a production line we had to get the place cleaned up after every meal.

Waiters and waitresses brought their trays to a counter were Dan Finneran unloaded them. Norma Miller (who later became the wife of my roommate, Wally Higgins) "swazzled" each dish, which meant that she hand washed it in a big pot of water. (Our dishwashing machine, although new, didn't perform as well as it should have.) I then loaded the dishes in racks and ran them through the dishwasher, and slid the racks out onto another counter to dry in the air. Waiters and waitresses put the dishes back in the cabinets after they had cleared their tables.

Once in a while on a Friday or Saturday night, when a lot of the diners didn't show up and we had surplus waiters or waitresses, I'd announce a Clorox party. That meant that every single dish was taken from the shelves, plunged into big kettles of bleach, and then put through the washer. The whole place smelled of chlorine those nights.

Our pay was free meals, so all of us working in the kitchen and dining room ate earlier than the "guests," and I think Joe, the main cook, gave us the best cuts of meat and generous servings of everything, including his home-made pies.

Things were usually peaceful in the kitchen except for raucous laughter from the sink where George Busby entertained everybody with wonderfully funny stories while he scrubbed the pots and pans.

On one occasion there was a bit of excitement. A student burst in, came over to me, and said he was going to beat me up right there beside the dishwasher for something I had printed in the *Fiat Lux*. He had been in a minor traffic accident and we had used a one-paragraph item. For some reason he was afraid his mother would see the story.

As our voices rose above the rumble of the dishwasher a few people collected around us, including Joe, who brought along one of his razor-sharp long knives. The guy who was giving me the trouble spotted the knife and the determined look on Joe's face and took off. I never saw him again.

After my freshman year I had to move out of Bartlett Dormitory, which was only for freshmen. Three friends and I rented a room in an old house owned by the university controller. Our second-floor room was heated, like many in Alfred, by a little open gas heater. We were always afraid to leave it burning during the night in case the wind from an open window blew out the flame. Gary insisted that a window be wide open while we slept.

At night the last guy to bed turned off the heater, hoisted a window up and propped it open with a stick. It wouldn't stay up unless the stick was in position.

Gary was always the first one up in the morning so his job was to try to close the window and light the heater. He pulled the stick out of the open window, but the sash was usually frozen open and wouldn't close. He lit the heater anyway because at least one of the rest of us was awake and could watch to see that the flame didn't get blown out. Eventually the room warmed up enough to melt the ice holding the window open and it came down with a resounding crash. Poor Mr. Crump downstairs with that noise overhead every morning.

In my junior and senior years I lived in the Burdick Hall, an upperclassmen's dormitory over the Student Union. Burdick was an antique wooden structure with a great wide-open stairway in the center. I thought it was a great firetrap, and sure enough, one summer after I had graduated it went up in flames. No one was living there at the time, and the university was rid of a hazard and eyesore.

Don't get the idea that Alfred was all pranks, quirky professors, stiff necked churchmen, and quaint customs. It had all those things, but also provided an excellent education. My four years at Alfred flew past in a flash. I still think about them, especially when I get alumni association reports. They were some of the best years of my life.

Chapter 15

A FEW LEFTOVERS

W hen I'm reading the last few pages of some books I want the story to continue forever. Other books I'm glad to finish so I can lay them aside. Which category this volume falls into is, of course, for you to decide.

I could paraphrase the Episcopal Church's *Book of Common Prayer:* "I have written those things that I ought not to have written and left unwritten those things that I ought to have written." That's not quite the way they say it in the church; but you can look it up yourself.

Whatever I "ought not to have written" I'll let stand, but as for what "I ought to have written" I'll add a few things yet.

Grease Walker. How did he get that name? His real name was Harold. As for how the change came about, all I can do is repeat the story my dad told me. He said that he and Harold and a couple of their friends, all probably in their early 20s, were wandering around Olcott Beach one summer day. I suppose they were trying to pick up some girls. I doubt if Harold ever had a date in his life (other than with Aunt Bert, the sacrificial lamb, on Christmas Day), so I expect that he was all excited and talking constantly. That part of his personality didn't change as he grew older.

These gallant young men apparently weren't having much success with finding girls, so wandered down to the docks to look at the yachts and motorboats in the water. They could dream about having one someday. (None ever did.) They were dressed like millionaire boat owners in white suits, colorful ties, and sporty flat-top straw hats.

From here on the story is unclear, but somehow Harold ended up in the water. Whether he fell (doubtful) or was pushed (more likely) was never really spelled out. At any rate, the shallow water where he plunged in was covered with floating oil and gasoline from the boats, and Harold emerged from his dip nicely coated with the sludge. His white suit and straw hat were ruined.

How he got dried off and back home was never discussed either, but for evermore Harold was known as "Grease" Walker. Evermore until about 20 years later when his mother finally heard the story and misunderstood the name. "You called him *Greasy?*" she asked, unable to believe it. From then on Harold had another nickname—Greasy.

I don't know how Lester Fulston, my father's uncle, became Tonius, but I should relate how Tonius added his name to the lexicon of gastronomy. Tonius was often at our house for a meal or an after-dinner snack, usually in the company of Aunt Lilly and Uncle Art.

The meal or snack often wound down with a bit of my mother's home-made dessert, fruit cake around the holidays, maybe a pie at other times, or sometimes just some of her big white and molasses cookies. She always put extra dessert on the table so that at the end of the meal there was an extra slice or two of fruit cake, a piece of pie or a few cookies that nobody seemed to be able to eat.

Conversation at the table went on, and then Tonius quietly slid out his knife and cut a tiny slice off the extra dessert. "I'll just eat a little corner of that," he said and polished it off. More conversation and maybe another cup of tea followed. Eventually Tonius' knife sneaked out again and he carved another bit off the dessert. In a few minutes he said, "There's no sense in leaving that last little piece." He ate it too. All of the leftover dessert would now have disappeared. This method of eating by degrees became known as Toniusing. He absolutely would not have taken the whole piece at one time; it had to be Toniused.

Tonius was so quiet he'd often be overlooked, especially if Greasy and his mother were holding forth at full volume. I never knew whether Tonius ever had a girlfriend and if he did why they had never married. It was just always assumed that Tonius was to be forever single, live with the Blossers, sleep in a little low-ceilinged bedroom up a stairway where anyone taller than him always bumped their head on the ceiling.

My parents thought Tonius' life must have been lonely, so they sometimes took him with us on vacations to the Thousand Islands in the St. Lawrence River or New York's

Adirondack State Park, where we'd get a housekeeping cabin with three bedrooms.

At the Thousand Islands Tonius, my dad and I fished off the dock in front of the cabin or rowed a little way out into the river. We caught tiny perch too small to keep, but it was fun. After the little fish had stripped the bait off Tonius' hook he kept the bare hook in the water while he pulled down the brim of his straw hat and slept.

In front of our cabin on one vacation chipmunks scurried about while Tonius fed them peanuts in the shell. After a while Tonius wondered what would happen if he just gave the chipmunks an empty peanut shell. They rejected it. Then Tonius tied pieces of an empty shell together with string. This was very delicate work, to get two halves of a shell that hadn't been smashed, to make them fit closely together and then to tie the shell together with a bit of string and make a tiny knot. He put a tiny pebble inside the empty shell so that it rattled and weighed about the same as a regular peanut. Tonius, having nothing more pressing to do, worked at this artistic endeavor until he thought it would fool Mr. Chipmunk. It didn't. The chipmunk took one look at Tonius' handiwork and threw the empty shell at him.

Vacations were trips in the car, usually to a destination we could reach in one day, but sometimes we drove through New England or the Catskill Mountains of southern New York. During the wartime gasoline rationing the trips had to be short, and we stayed in one cabin the whole week. Gasoline ration coupons were saved by not using the car much for the weeks before the vacation.

We cooked all of our meals while on a trip. For a while a charcoal grill was used, but it was an unhandy thing when we were in a hurry, so once my dad borrowed a gasoline stove from someone. We were in a pine forest when he first tried to light it. He pumped up pressure in the gas tank, adjusted a couple of valves, and struck a match. Whoosh! Flames shot up higher than the lowest branches of the trees, but fortunately they didn't catch fire.

He turned off the stove, and it was never used again. He got in the car and drove to the nearest village. In an hour or so he came back with a metal box that looked like a small suitcase. When opened, it revealed itself as a new two-burner gasoline stove that could stand on one end of the picnic table.

He pumped the tank, twisted the valves, struck a match, and there was a quiet blue flame that was just right to fit under the pan my mother had been waiting to cook in. No flames shot into the trees, and my dad said the best part was that the stove was very cheap. We took it with us on vacations and picnics for years.

At least once almost every summer weekend we had a picnic somewhere. Often they were at Olcott Beach on Lake Ontario. In the fall we went to parks south of Buffalo, where the hills were a blaze of colors, and on very hot days or evenings drove a couple of miles to Outwater Park in Lockport, where we could get cooled off and escape George Kastner's car painting fumes.

Quite often we took either Jimmy or Howard Garlock with us. I guess my folks thought that if I had another kid to play with I wouldn't be bugging them to do things with me. Two kids could go on the teeter-totter, climb on the jungle gym, and go down the slide on a piece of wax paper (a bread wrapper) to make the slide slippery. I was never crazy about swings. If I went too high or fast in one, I began to be nauseated.

Taking one of the Garlocks along worked out well for everyone. Jimmy or Howard wouldn't have gone anywhere without us, since no one in their house had a car; my parents could relax because I had a friend to play with; I had a better time, and Mrs. Garlock unloaded at least one kid for a few hours.

Once or twice a year we took an excursion to a park in nearby Canada. The two main Canadian destinations were Crystal Beach on Lake Erie or Port Dalhousie on Lake Ontario. We pronounced Dalhousie as Duh-Loozey, which I somehow doubt was the correct way. Both places were big amusement parks with broad sandy beaches. The water was warm and clear and we could walk for what seemed like a mile into the lakes without getting wet above our knees.

Unfortunately for me, but fortunately for my dad's wallet, the amusement rides were almost all closed. It was Sunday, and Ontario had strict blue laws about amusements. Maybe there could be a little kiddy ride that made no noise but certainly nothing beyond that.

Even though the amusement rides at the Canadian parks were closed on Sunday, the only day we could go because my dad worked six days a week, there were rides at Olcott

Beach. I liked the bump cars best, but there was also a small Ferris wheel, an ornate merry-go-round where bigger kids and adults could grab for rings as they rode by, and a few rides for little kids. There were games as well—ski-ball, bottles to knock down with baseballs, and targets to shoot at with pop guns.

We parked the car on Main Street in Olcott (angle parking to get the best view of the pedestrians) and watched to see who was walking up and down. We did that on Main Street in Lockport, too. Was I ever bored! If it was daylight, I took along a comic book to read. Sometimes as a reward we got ice cream cones at Castle's, the Olcott branch of the big ice cream parlor near Lockport High School.

A few times we took a major excursion to an amusement park at Canandaigua on one of New York's picturesque Finger Lakes. This excursion was all of 80 miles, *each way,* even longer than the annual trek in the Toniusmobile to visit one of his relatives near Rochester.

The trip to Canandaigua required several days of planning. It may have even required an oil change and greasing of the car and possibly replacement of a tire. It was too far (and expensive) to take one of the Garlocks along. The amusement rides cost serious money. There was even miniature golf, and we all played at who knows what expense.

My folks liked the gardens all around the park and the many rows of benches in front of a bandstand where there were frequent free concerts. Even though Lockport was "the center of the universe," it had nothing to compare to the park at Canandaigua.

My parents weren't the only ones who undertook long journeys. Their friends, Hamer and Eunice Brown, came to visit often, especially when they had to report that the following day they'd "drive through" to Olean, New York, a trek of 80 miles.

I never heard anyone else say they were going to "drive through" to anywhere, but we in Lockport may have had a private language of our own. The Browns, when they weren't intent on "driving through," would go to the country for "a jag of wood." In our house we burned coal in the furnace, which left behind "clinkers" of ashes that had to be hauled outside behind the "pie plant" (rhubarb) and sifted. Near the pie plant grew the "flags" (irises.)

That furnace, by the way, provided hot water as well as heat, but during the months when there was no fire in the furnace, water was heated in other ways. To wash dishes or for my father's shaving, a teakettle was heated on the kitchen stove. But for a bath the gas heater in the cellar had to be lighted. That was a scary undertaking. The gas was turned on, then a lighted match was held inside near the pipes. Suddenly there was a small explosion of flame. I always expected the heater to blow up.

By the way, anything below ground was a cellar, none of that basement business that people talk about out in the interior of the country. The word is cellar, at least it always was for us.

On the way upstairs from the cellar after the near conflagration with the water heater I probably had to take some potatoes for my mother who was waiting to fry them in the "spider," (a big, black, cast-iron frying pan). When the potatoes were served they were dotted with "oleo" (margarine) which was white and came in a plastic bag along with a dot of red dye. The oleo had to be kneaded inside the plastic bag to mix it with the color. All of this nonsense was some sort of law that the dairy lobby had foisted on us in the hopes that we'd use butter instead of oleo.

If we got constipation from the potatoes and oleo, we took a dose of "physic" (laxative.) My dad had the idea that he and I needed a daily dose of "physic," so every night we took a tablespoon of mineral oil mixed with an equal amount of some kind of fruit juice. For some reason the juice from the home-canned pears always seemed the best way to camouflage the oil, which really had no taste, but was thick and made me gag.

Greasey's car had something that has long since vanished—a rumble seat. That was an open air seat behind the closed cab of the car, where the trunk is now on modern cars. The rumble seat was sometimes called the mother-in-law seat, but since Greasey had no mother-in-law, nor anyone else to ride in the seat, it was never used.

I didn't have a car, of course, but my dad would give me orders to go to the store on my "wheel" (bicycle) to get him a couple of cigars. He'd give me a penny for "penny candy," and that one cent would actually buy two or three large pieces of something.

Back in the old days he started his car with a "crank," a handle out in front that had to be turned vigorously to get the engine running. In deep snow he put "lugs" (chains) on the rear tires for better traction.

Roads had their own system of identification, too. From Lockport when we headed toward Buffalo, we went up *the* Transit, then up *the* Millersport Highway. Out in the country we used *the* Rounds Road, *the* Brown Road, *the* Ewings Road, or maybe even *the* Checkered Tavern Road. We used up a lot of *the*s, but there seemed to be a lot of them, and people in Niagara County were ever generous—except when it came to giving votes to Democrats. Of course, in the city, *the*s were few and far between. We never lived on *the* Waterman Street or went to visit Tonius on *the* Bristol Avenue. Just one of those strange things, I guess.

I suppose we ate things that would now be considered peculiar. Like limburger cheese sandwiches. My mother liked rhubarb soup and sour cherry soup with dumplings in it. Both were served cold. We had cookies for breakfast, fatty wieners and hamburgers, iced tea mixed with ginger ale (try it), and often made a whole meal of either corn or strawberries when in season. The berries were served over my mother's freshly made baking powder biscuits. The best beans were baked in the wood-fired oven, not in the Boy Scout hole of dirt; and potatoes were also best when baked near a coal or wood fire. Of course there were all kinds of casseroles made with canned soups, but they can be overlooked. We didn't know any better.

Once in a while my mother served Spam, an awful canned meat made of ham and God knows what else. I thought it was some food substitute invented during World War II, but I guess it went back into the 30s. It is still sold, but I can't for the life of me figure out why.

There were also some foods, now common, that we never had at our house. Like pizza. Never even heard of it. And spaghetti. The first time I had that was when I was invited to David Palmer's house for supper. His father was a Baptist minister, and, I suppose, grossly underpaid. They probably served spaghetti because it was cheap. I didn't even know how to eat it and had to be taught. Back home I told my parents about that wonderful food I'd just had and asked if we could have it at our house. My mother said "yes," but we never had any.

The Palmers lived in a huge house on Locust Street. The place had two-story white pillars, grand high-ceilinged drawing rooms and bedrooms that wouldn't quit. The only trouble was that the Palmers couldn't afford to heat or furnish many of the rooms. David and I used whole rooms to set up our electric trains. We operated them while we wore our winter coats. I suppose the church might have inherited the big mansion, and not being able to sell it, turned it into a parsonage. To make ends meet, the minister sold eggs during the week.

In Lockport in the 1930s and 40s we had our own vocabulary, foods, and life style, but I don't suppose anyone would understand much of any of it today. Gone is the ice box, the ice man, the bread and milk deliveries, most of the little corner groceries, the farms where we could buy raw milk and the quiet back roads where beginning drivers could practice their art in safety.

Perhaps also gone (but I hope not) is the freedom I had to ride my bike all over Lockport, up and down narrow streets where the houses nearly projected onto the pavement, past very elaborate and stately grand homes, and through parks to watch fat men try to play softball. I could explore the Italian neighborhoods in the west end of the city and the small black area in Lowertown (if I wanted to cope with the big hill). I always felt perfectly safe, except maybe when a dog might chase my bike, but the owners usually called it off before there was any confrontation.

Gone, at least for now, is the Great Depression, which we all hope never appears again. Wars haven't ended and probably never will, but Americans' involvement on the home front in World War II was something we've never seen since.

Of the Lockport I knew, even though much remains the same, there are changes everywhere, some for the better, others to be regretted. I guess Joyce Carol Oates is right. Remembering Lockport is like looking at a sepia-tone photo. Just the same, it was a great place to grow up in the 1930s and 40s. I hope it still is for the current generation.

Chapter 16

EVERYTHING GETS RELATIVE HERE

y children got me into writing this memoir, and they may be interested in learning more about their ancestors, but I doubt if anyone else is. This chapter is for the kids. The rest of you can go out for a beer if you want to. There was a perfectly decent ending to the book in the last chapter, so you could have quit there, but if you stick around you could get answers to some things that may have been puzzling you since we launched off together.

You've met my father's Uncle Tonius. He never married, and in all the pictures of him in my family photo album he is always the same age, somewhere between 50 and 60. He always wore a hat pulled low over his face so he could lounge in a chair and sleep when he thought no one would be watching.

Tonius wasn't his real name, but almost everybody called him that. His name was Lester Fulston. That's where my dad and I got our middle names. I have no idea where he got the name of Tonius. It probably went back into ancient history—my family's ancient history, not that stuff about the fall of Rome, etc. Tonius had a sister, Grace, who was the Aunt Grace that my father lived with as a kid after his father died and his mother went into a hospital, but Aunt Grace died before I was born.

Tonius lived with another sister, Lillian Blosser, (Aunt Lilly to me) and her husband, Art. Aunt Lilly never learned to drive, and Uncle Art was too excitable to ever risk his life behind the wheel, so Tonius was the "designated driver" before anyone ever heard of that expression. I think he spent half of his life sitting in the car outside the Baptist church in Lockport waiting for Aunt Lilly to come out of one of her many meetings. Lockport wasn't so big that Tonius couldn't have gone back home, but he didn't. He sat in the car, smoked a cigar and took a nap. Cars didn't have radios in those days, at least Tonius' and ours didn't.

Uncle Art worked for the gas company—Lockport Light, Heat and Power. He probably got a discount on gas appliances, which is the reason that his house had a gas-powered refrigerator, the only one I have ever seen. And the cook stoves in Aunt Lilly's kitchen and in ours were monsters apparently designed by someone who wasn't wholly convinced that gas fuel was here to stay.

Each stove had two ovens, one gas-fired and the other wood-burning. There was a gas- fired broiler, separate from the oven, and two sets of burners, one set using gas and the other set over the wood fire. The monster stoves were made of what looked like cast iron and took up almost as much room in the kitchen as two modern stoves. Ours was so heavy that it began making the kitchen floor sag, forcing my dad to put a steel post in the basement to shore it up. My folks dared not get rid of the monster stove, though. What would Uncle Art say? And, to be truthful, that wood burning part of the stove was very handy during a winter blizzard when the power went off.

I don't know what finally pushed my dad over the edge, but he somehow screwed his courage to the sticking point, as Lady Macbeth said, and got somebody to haul away the monster of the kitchen and replace it with a neat, white electric range. Uncle Art never let a peep out of him, and I suspect Aunt Lilly began telling him that they ought to do the same thing in their kitchen, but they never did.

My father, an only child, by the way, had another aunt, Emily Bayliss, and a cousin, Evelyn Bayliss, but we didn't see them as often as we did the Blossers and Uncle Tonius. Assuredly, it was a pitifully small family

A few years ago I decided I'd like to know more about my ancestors and started tracing them. I got back to my great-great grandfather, John Bredell. He was born in London, England, in 1803 and moved to Lockport, New York, in 1845 and opened a store at the corner of Elm and Main. His wife was named Sarah, and they had a son, John

Mountain Bredell (there are a lot of Johns and Franks among the Bredells.)

The Civil War was none of John M. Bredell's business, of course, but nevertheless, he enlisted in the Union Army and was captured twice and held in southern prison camps. All this I've taken from the obituary that appeared in the Lockport newspaper in 1889. Here's more:

> *"His army service left him in poor health and while he has been able to work more or less since he came home he has never been a well man and suffered to a great extent. For a long time he has not been able to lie down to any extent and died in a sitting posture. He was a gentleman who was highly respected by his comrades and his demise will be regretted by all."*

There was no report in the newspaper of what, if anything, John M. Bredell did for a living, although a book published in 1921 said he had a grocery. Maybe it was the one his father had started. He died at age 58. His wife, Elizabeth A. Day, of Lockport, lived to be 84. Her father had come from England, and her mother, Catherine Halpern, from Ireland. See, I do have a bit of the Old Sod in me.

John M. and his wife had three children, my father's uncle, Frank M. Bredell; his aunt, Emily M. Bayliss; and his father, Ellis M. Bredell, my grandfather. I never knew "Great Uncle Frank" (Frank M.), who died when I was little, but my father often talked about him in reverential terms. Great Uncle Frank was once postmaster of Lockport, held other civic offices such as jury commissioner and supervisor, and was a founder of the Niagara Baking Co., where my dad worked.

Lockport city directories for part of the 1890's list my grandfather, Ellis Bredell, as a shirt cutter who lived at 168 Pound Street. He died at age 44. My father was only eight. Three years later his mother, Minnie E. Fulston Bredell, was committed to Buffalo State Hospital, a mental institution, where she died several years later.

Here's where some of the mysteries come in. I had always assumed that she had died when my dad was young and that he didn't remember her, but in fact she lived in the hospital until he was 15. He must have remembered her but never mentioned her name. Why? Shame because she was in a mental hospital?

I never knew anything about her until recently when I got a copy of her death certificate from the New York State health department. She died of lobar pneumonia and carcinoma of the breast, recurrent after some operation, the death certificate says. It lists manic depression as a contributing factor.

I guess it must have been an awful trauma for my father to think that his mother died in a mental hospital. He just couldn't bring himself to mention her and never gave any hint about her or his father. The only earlier relative he'd talk about was Uncle Frank.

Dad gave out some clues to what he knew, but I wasn't smart enough to pick them up. When I'd get to acting up, he'd warn me that if I didn't behave "they'd put me Up in Buffalo." I suppose "Up in Buffalo" meant the state hospital, but I never caught on. I just thought it was small town jealousy of the big city.

In Chestnut Ridge Cemetery, east of Lockport, is a monument (a large stone marking several graves) with the name Bredell on it, and one of the graves is that of Frank M.

At age 51 he married Anna Elizabeth Dempsey. It was a late marriage, so the question arises, was there an earlier one? His obituary made no mention of an earlier spouse. You'd expect Anna Elizabeth Dempsey to be buried next to her husband, but she isn't. She's not even in the same cemetery but way across town in a Catholic cemetery owned by St. Patrick's Church. My guess is that she (or some relatives) wanted her to be buried in a cemetery consecrated by the Catholic Church, and Chestnut Ridge does not fill the bill. Hence, she and her husband were separated in death.

There is still another mystery related to Anna Dempsey Bredell. She lived until I was about 23 or 24 years old, but I hardly heard of her when I was a kid, and when I did it was just the name Dempsey with no indication that she was related or even still alive. We never went to visit her. Why not? Were my parents so bigoted that they wouldn't associate with Catholics? I don't think so. My best friends were Catholics.

While my dad was a "city slicker," my mother was a farm girl who came to the big city of Lockport to work in a bank as a young woman. I don't know how or when my mother and dad met. My earliest photos of them were taken in 1928, when they had already married and built the house at 238 Waterman Street where I grew up.

My mother's parents, Fred and Ida Cramp, were farmers who worked the land on shares. That means that they did the work on someone else's farm and lived in a rented farmhouse. Whatever profits there were got divided between land owner and tenant farmer. They moved often in a small circle of farms north of Lockport. The only one of those farms I can remember bordered on Lake Ontario. From the ramshackle house you could walk for about ten minutes through fields and apple orchards and end up on the stony beach of the frigid lake.

Fred Cramp and Ida (Seelow) Cramp came from Germany as children and were married in this country. I've been able to trace the family tree back to Fred Cramp's parents (my great-grandparents), John F. Cramp and his wife Louise Hausen, or Hansen (the handwriting isn't clear), both of whom were born in Germany in the early 1830's. The family name was originally spelled Krampe, then somebody dropped the final e, and someone else changed it to Cramp, probably because they didn't want to appear to be so German.

My grandfather died when I was three, so I remember him only from his pictures. My mother told me that in addition to farming, he was the superintendent of Krull Park at Olcott Beach and made certain that there was no roughhousing, no papers on the grass and that everyone behaved properly. People were scared to disobey him.

Even though he'd been in this country most of his life, he could probably read German better than English and subscribed to a German newspaper. During World War I people thought he must have been a German spy. What would he be spying on? Apple trees or picnickers?

My mother had two brothers, Norman and Wilfred (who was always called Butz) and two sisters, Gertrude and Bertha. My mother was the oldest. Many writers would say that my grandmother's house, the one I remember, was a rambling old farmhouse. It was like a lot of others on Niagara County farms, two stories high with a steeply pitched roof, a kind of L-shaped floor plan with a little porch in the notch of the L. The front door, or at least the one we used all the time, led into a big dining room with a round table and lots of old-fashioned chairs. There was a wood-burning stove for heat.

Behind the dining room was an old-fashioned kitchen. The sink had a wooden drain board, and drinking water came from a pump outside in the yard. There was a pump in the kitchen, but it only brought up rainwater that was stored in the cistern in the basement and was just used for washing. The stove was a monster-sized wood burning affair. No gas ovens or burners there. I remember my grandmother stoking it with big chunks of wood from diseased apple trees that had been cut down.

The dining room was also the sitting room with a couple of couches and a collection of worn upholstered chairs. To the left of the dining room was a parlor, never used and not heated and filled with uncomfortable looking and long outdated furniture and big dull pictures. It had a piano, however, which my cousins and I used to pound on mercilessly until the noise got so bad that somebody made us stop and go outside. The floor plan of the house was such that we could chase each other around through the kitchen, the hall next to the unheated bedrooms, the parlor and back into the dining room. The only problem was that we had to dodge the hot stove in the dining room and the even hotter stove in the kitchen during winter visits. We could chase each other around the circuit only once or twice, slamming doors as we went, before we were again expelled from the house.

I think the upper story of the house was really more of an attic than usable space. I don't remember ever going up there. I did go into the cellar, a pit under at least part of the house with rough stone walls and a dirt floor. It was entered via barn-type doors outside the house, and was only used for storing potatoes, turnips, carrots, cabbage and apples. There were no windows, and it was damp and cold, even in the summer, but a good place to store the crops.

Out in back of the house were the pump, woodpile, barn and outhouse. The outhouse came equipped with the requisite Sears-Roebuck catalogue, not for use, but to read. Not much reading was done in the outhouse, though. In winter it was freezing and in summer the flies buzzed. I tried not to visit it if I could hold out.

My grandmother contracted diabetes and went blind at age 52. She also had an infection in one foot that wouldn't heal and had a toe amputated. The infection spread, and ultimately she lost one leg and had to walk on crutches for 25 years. She had a wooden leg, but it was only for looks and was no good to walk on. She also was quite deaf and had a couple kinds of antique "hearing aids." One was an ear trumpet, a little metal shell-like device with a stem that went into her ear. She had to hold it up to one ear to use it. It would probably have done as much good if she had held up a cow horn or a seashell to her ear. We screamed into the horn, but she still couldn't hear much of what we tried to tell her.

The other device was like a telephone earpiece attached to what looked like the hose of a vacuum cleaner. She'd put the earphone over one ear and aim the vacuum cleaner hose at whoever she thought was talking. That was totally useless, but you can't imagine how agile she had to be to keep pointing the thing at the proper speaker during a conversation that she could neither hear nor see. I think somebody got the device at the Salvation Army store. My grandmother gamely gave it a good try, but it soon went into the junk and was never seen again. Too bad. It would be an interesting antique now.

Her son, my uncle, Butz, was working the farm, keeping a few cows and growing cabbage, apples and maybe some other crops. The farm didn't make enough money to live on, though, so he also had a job in a steel mill in Lockport, about 30 to 40 minutes drive away. My aunt Bertha kept the house. Before she went blind my grandmother helped on the farm and also was the janitor at the one-room school across the road, going over early in the morning to light a fire in the coal stove every day.

Finally all this got to be too much, and they moved to Newfane, a little village about eight miles away. My grandmother sat on the porch and sewed together long strips of rags which were then woven by somebody into rugs. The rugs were sold and brought in a little money, but mostly the sewing of the rags just gave her something to do besides listening to the radio (a push button when such devices were rare) and the talking books, which were large 78 rpm records, played on a small phonograph next to her bed.

The minister of her church sometimes came to call on her and brought tape recordings of his recent sermons, which she listened to politely. Since her eyes were always closed by blindness, he couldn't tell whether she was asleep unless she snored.

So there you have a little information about my ancestors. There is a chart on the next page that may help straighten things out, or confuse you. At least I have spared you from a super-sized chart that would list all of my cousins and their spouses, children, grandchildren and great grandchildren. When my dad got confused by family members, or more likely had had too much of them, he categorize them all as "your foolish relation." Never his "foolish relation," always "yours." Mine? They were his too.

MY FAMILY TREE

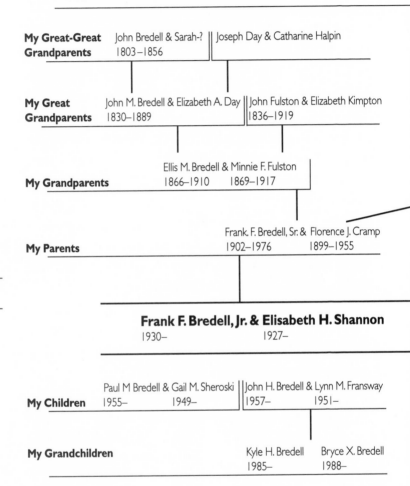

My Great-Great Grandparents John Bredell & Sarah-? ‖ Joseph Day & Catharine Halpin
1803–1856

My Great Grandparents John M. Bredell & Elizabeth A. Day ‖ John Fulston & Elizabeth Kimpton
1830–1889 1836–1919

My Grandparents Ellis M. Bredell & Minnie F. Fulston
1866–1910 1869–1917

My Parents Frank. F. Bredell, Sr. & Florence J. Cramp
1902–1976 1899–1955

Frank F. Bredell, Jr. & Elisabeth H. Shannon
1930– 1927–

My Children Paul M Bredell & Gail M. Sheroski ‖ John H. Bredell & Lynn M. Fransway
1955– 1949– 1957– 1951–

My Grandchildren Kyle H. Bredell Bryce X. Bredell
1985– 1988–

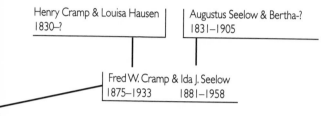

Henry Cramp & Louisa Hausen
1830–?

Augustus Seelow & Bertha-?
1831–1905

Fred W. Cramp & Ida J. Seelow
1875–1933   1881–1958

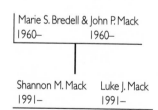

Marie S. Bredell & John P. Mack
1960–   1960–

Shannon M. Mack   Luke J. Mack
1991–   1991–

ABOUT THE AUTHOR

Frank Bredell started his professional career in journalism while a junior and senior at Alfred University, getting paid the magnificent sum of 10 cents for every inch of what he wrote that appeared in such newspapers as the *Buffalo Evening News, Rochester Democrat & Chronicle, Olean Times Herald, Elmira Star-Gazette, Hornell Evening Tribune* and *Wellsville Daily Reporter*, not to mention three newswire services that paid a dime for every sports score and news tip.

With all that money pouring in, the writer became hooked on journalism as a career and after graduating from Alfred received a master's degree from the Columbia University Graduate School of Journalism in New York City.

With his degree in hand he skipped over the usual small town start of a career in newspapering and went directly to a metropolitan daily, if you consider Buffalo, NY, a metropolis.

Unfortunately, the newspaper, the *Courier-Express,* is no longer with us, but he could in no way be blamed for its demise, having left several years earlier to join the editorial staff of *The Detroit News.*

After a dozen years of wielding a newspaper editor's black (not blue as everyone believes) pencil, the author took up a career in public relations, working for a PR agency, Harper-Grace Hospitals in Detroit, and finally operating his own business in Lincoln Park, Michigan. As the year 2000 approached he gave up working because he no longer had time for it. There were too many other interesting things to do, places to go and articles to write.

TRAVEL MEMORIES
by Frank Bredell

African Safari—Up close with lions, elephants, zebras, wildebeests, hippos, etc.; elegant hotels in the African back country; visits to "Stone Age" Masai and Samburu villages; a hot-air balloon ride over the Serengeti Plain; the dust, rough roads and lure of Africa—a land that will never let me go.

Exploring the Ancient Marvels of Mexico—Visits to the intriguing Mayan, Aztec, Toltec pyramids at Chichen Itza, Uxmal, Palenque, Mitla and Monte Alban; the glorious gold-filled church at Oaxaca, fascinating Mexico City, plus my encounter with what may be the worst hotel in Mexico.

Touring Greece, the Land of the Gods—The partially restored 8000-year-old city of Knossos on Crete, exploring Santorini (the lost Atlantis?), the one-time slave-trading island of Delos, being held prisoner by the ocean on Naxos, the Parthenon in ancient Athens and adventures in dining.

Unlocking the Secrets of Turkey—Exotic Istanbul, modern Ankara, the "moonscape" of Cappadocia, following the footsteps of St. Paul, the Turquoise Coast, site of the Trojan War and where Homer had the key to history, the ancient city of Ephesus and the house where St. Mary lived.

Exploring Germany—Berlin, Dresden, Hamburg, Leipzig, Lubeck, Frankfurt, Oberamergau, Heidelberg, the castles of Crazy King Ludwig, Munich's best beer hall, a cruise on the Rhine and much more.

Meandering with Michael—A visit to Tunisia, unknown to most Americans, but home to the world's best museum of mosaics, mosques that rival those in Mecca, twisting alleys of medinas and souks, the mysterious Atlas Mountains, and camel rides across the Sahara.

Exploring Below the Equator—A tour of South Africa with visits to Victoria Falls in Zimbabwe, Botswana and the tiny kingdom of Swaziland, where the sights and sounds of the reborn southern Africa vie with traditional village life.

Journals in preparation:

♦ A journey through Eastern Eurorpe, especially romantic Vienna, Prague and Budapest. You'll want to read this memoir while you sip a glass of wine and listen to some waltzes.

♦ Visiting India, a nation of contrasts, from the incomparable Taj Mahal to the ancient temples at Mahabalipuram.

All journals are $10.95 plus $2 postage and handling.

Order from **Andiamo Press,** *Box 484, Lincoln Park, MI 48146*
e-mail: Fbredell@aol.com

This book was set mostly in Adobe Caslon and Gill Sans typefaces.
Type was set by John Cole Graphic Designer,
of Santa Fe, New Mexico,
and the book was printed and bound
by McNaughton & Gunn, Inc., of Saline, Michigan.